Life After ...
Engineering and
Built Environment

Thousands of students graduate from university each year. The lucky few have the rest of their lives mapped out in perfect detail – but for most, things are not nearly so simple. Armed with your hard-earned degree the possibilities and career paths lying before you are limitless, and the number of choices you suddenly have to make can seem bewildering.

Life After ... Engineering and Built Environment has been written specifically to help students currently studying, or who have recently graduated, make informed choices about their future lives. It will be a source of invaluable advice and wisdom to graduates (whether you wish to use your degree directly or not), covering such topics as:

* Identifying a career path that interests you – and how to start pursuing it
* The worldwide opportunities open to engineering graduates
* Staying motivated and pursuing your goals
* Networking and self-promotion
* Making the transition from scholar to worker
* Putting the skills you have developed at university to good use in life

The *Life After ...* series of books are more than simple 'career guides'. They are unique in taking a holistic approach to career advice – recognising the increasing view that, although a successful working life is vitally important, other factors can be just as essential to happiness and fulfilment. They are *the* indispensible handbooks for students considering their future directionin life.

Sally Longson is a life coach and well-known writer and media commentator in the field of careers.

Also available from Sally Longson

Life After ... Art and Design
0-415-37590-8

Life After ... Business and Administrative Studies
0-415-37591-6

Life After ... Language and Literature
0-415-37593-2

Life After ... Engineering and Built Environment

A practical guide to life after your degree

Sally Longson

LONDON AND NEW YORK

First published 2006
by Routledge
2 Park Square, Milton Park, Abingdon, Oxon OX14 4RN

Simultaneously published in the USA and Canada
by Routledge
711 Third Avenue, New York, NY 10017

Routledge is an imprint of the Taylor & Francis Group, an informa business

© 2006 Sally Longson

Typeset in Sabon by
HWA Text and Data Management, Tunbridge Wells

British Library Cataloguing in Publication Data
A catalogue record for this book is available from the British Library

Library of Congress Cataloging-in-Publication Data
Longson, Sally
   Life after – engineering and built environment: a practical guide to
   life after your degree / Sally Longson. – 1st ed.
     p.   cm.
   Includes bibliographical references and index.
   1. Vocational guidance.   2. College graduates – Employment
     3. Career development.
   I. Title.   II. Title: Practical guide to life after your degree.
   HF5381.L6574 2006
   650.1–dc22   2006001067

ISBN10: 0–415–37592–4
ISBN10: 0–203–08843–3
ISBN13: 978–0–415–37592–4

Contents

Preface

Your degree over – or nearly over – you contemplate your next move, rather like a game of chess. You plot your next move, you fall into it, or someone makes you fall into it. Life is continually like a game of chess, but check-mate is entirely where you – or someone else – decides where it is to be. You can plan to move forward and make progress, or you can feel like a pawn, moved around a board at someone else's bidding.

There's plenty of good news about. A survey recently conducted by the Survey Shop and commissioned by the Royal Bank of Scotland provided optimistic results for you. Out of the 1,220 people polled who completed their studies in 2002, those who had gone into engineering were most satisfied – engineers had an overall score of 69 per cent, taking into account work–life balance, training and scope for promotion. The numbers of women in the sector are increasing – of nearly two million in the UK working in the construction industry, for example, 200,000 of them are women.

Engineering and the built environment sectors offer opportunities which are challenging and varied, and facilitate huge personal and career growth, whilst offering the chance to reach management levels at home and abroad. They also enable you to leave a true mark on the world and make a real difference, from the environment to space exploration, from the way we work, live and play to the way we travel. Your end results will bring you the satisfaction of knowing that you helped build something which will last for many years ahead. In short, you can make a real difference to the earth we inhabit and its wider place in space.

As engineers and built environment specialists, you have a very exciting future ahead indeed and one in which you can make a huge impact on the world, people and organisations around you. With your knowledge, skills and ability to pull projects together, you have the power to create a new world, more so than graduates of any other subject. Combine these with powerful business acumen and flair, creativity and inspiration, a firm eye on the bottom line and excellent interpersonal skills, the opportunities before you will be all the greater – if you create the right environment and recipe for success. In this ever smaller world, it is more important than ever for us all to be able to live and work across borders and to talk to and empathise with people from other countries. Add a working language or two to your portfolio of skills, and your world will explode with opportunities.

There are several tiers of skills demanded to succeed in the sector and get to the top, so look to develop them as your career progresses:

- technical expertise and knowledge;
- business acumen and understanding;
- interpersonal soft skills and the ability to handle people and motivate them.

The further you want to climb the career ladder in organisations, the more important the second and third will be, as you acquire posts in management, directorships and then, much later, appointments at Board level. Seek to push back the boundaries in all three within your own capabilities, just as you would push back boundaries of knowledge to invent a product. At all three levels, you're continually learning. The rules and regulations laid down by the professional bodies ensure that this is so. Yet should you decide to take your knowledge out of the sector, either immediately after your degree or later in your career, employers will welcome your ability to project manage, communicate, solve problems and lead teams.

The global economy has led employers to outsource huge amounts of work to other parts of the world and form partnerships, alliances and mergers with others to give them a global stage. It means that the country which secures the Olympic Games in 2016 may recruit engineers and construction workers from anywhere in the world. The lower skilled may come from local areas, but who knows where the companies with the contract, expertise and right sums to build stadiums, hotels, motorways and improve transport will come from. Be alert to the potential possibilities out there across the world; don't limit your horizons to home shores. Look out across the horizons before you and cast your mind and eyes beyond. And be ready to compete for career roles and contracts. Competing for your first employer and that all-important first role will be just the start.

Having a degree does not guarantee having a good job, although your prospects are better than most, particularly if you've got a good stint of work experience behind you. Nothing in life guarantees you a job. But there are key strategies you can enlist to enhance your chances of enjoying the career and life you want. This book will help you to identify them. You can continue to delve into its pages long after you graduate, because many of the exercises are designed to be timeless, enabling you to re-visit them in your life after your degree.

You may land yourself a job – but if you want a great job, you need to put persistent effort into ensuring that every day is a good day, that you're thinking long term and not to pay day and that you're giving back as opposed to just taking pay, perks and office coffee. Careers, like any relationships in life, need nurturing, and the hard work really only begins when you've started them. It is persistent hard work, which needs continual boosting, but it's worth it. Those who persist in their striving for a better career and life will succeed in enjoying one; those who give up along the way will take on a life which is of lesser quality than they could have and deserve. This is all the more important when you consider that there is expected to be a significant increase in the numbers of managers, professional occupations, association professional and technical occupations, and personal service occupations, especially in teaching and research and science, business and public service. The world is your oyster if you're prepared to put in the work for it and create your own luck.

A degree of humility and humbleness helps. You may be a graduate, but particularly if you are one without any work experience, you will need to be prepared to start at the beginning – or, to put it another way, the bottom – and work your way up. This is not an easy thing to acknowledge as you celebrate your new status as a degree holder, but such is life. Be passionate, be interested, be involved and be active. Ask questions, talk to people, be friendly and interested. They are where you may want to be.

Whatever stage you are at, a new graduate or someone who is about to graduate, now is a great time to assess your life and what you want out of it. Use the exercises in this book to help you determine just that. Careers are only part of life – there are a whole host of other things which are also important, such as relationships, finance and lifestyle. This book talks holistically about life after a degree, not just your career, although the main emphasis will be on career and work, because they affect many other areas of life. Head right out of your comfort zone and take risks to move on and make the most of your life ahead. Let's get started.

Chapter 1

Decisions, decisions ...

What happens now? What happens next?

What happens from now on depends on how determined you are to bring your hopes and aspirations, dreams and ambitions to fruition and the timescale within which you want to do it. Your future plans may be very clear to you, or you may be kicking lots of ideas about, or just not have a clue. What you *do* know is that there are lots of decisions to make and plans to be laid – but what, exactly? Where do you start?

Looking at the next few months

If you've already left university, you may have happily spent the summer enjoying a break at home before considering what happens next. The start of the academic year may feel strange as you realise that for the first time, perhaps in your life, you do not have to go back to school, college or university. You're free to do as you like. This may also be strange to the people you live with, such as your parents. They may not be used to you being around and may start giving you odd jobs to do which interfere with your day and which you may resent. Meal times may be punctuated with discussions about your future and when you're going to get a 'real' job and visitors to the house ask you about your plans. It may feel as though life is going backwards fast, instead of moving on to greater things. Build a structure into your life, even if you have no work or study to go to. Keeping to a routine now will help you when you start work.

You may have studied part time for your degree while holding down a full-time job, working two or three hours a night and trying the patience of family members as you disappear to study yet again. You've probably pleaded with the boss for more time off, spent lunch times doing research on the Internet and sneaked the odd sickie to get that assignment done. And now you're faced with many free hours and you feel a bit lost. It's nice to have a rest from all that study, but having risen to one challenge, you want another.

If you're still at university, create time *now* to plan your career. This involves participating in activities such as constructive work experience, internships, developing your web of industry contacts, voluntary work, attending careers and trade events and research into the job market, finding out what resources are available if you want to become self-employed, considering further study, visiting the careers service in person and online, and analysing your own strengths and capabilities. Allocate even three hours a week out of 168 during your degree, and you will be well on the road to securing your immediate future. You'll also have time to fill any missing gaps in your CV to strengthen any future job or course applications and make deadlines. If you are a post-graduate student, this equally applies. Visit your careers service to see how they can help you, and don't leave it too late.

Start building bridges from where you are now to where you want to be. The more foundations you can lay down now, the easier life will be later.

Take control. Get organised

Create a folder – call it something like 'Life After University' – and put everything you need to work on in it. It will save you time searching for pieces of paper and information. If you've got a PC or lap top, create a life and career folder on that, too, for emails and bookmark useful websites you visit regularly. Efficient organisation will clear your mind of clutter and enable you to work more effectively. Your 'life after' folder should grow week by week as you add to it and expand your knowledge, contacts, ideas and work.

Then look ahead

There are several key decisions to make about your life after graduating. These vary from the urgent and/or important, to those things which simply need to be dealt with, such as *'What will I do with all my books and materials?'* and *'Which friends do I want to keep in touch with?'* The latter two questions need to be cleared from your mind, to prevent them from muddying your thinking, so that you can focus on the all-important bigger picture.

There will be urgent decisions you need to make today. The important ones are not usually time pressured but they affect the Big Picture, i.e. your life. An important and urgent decision may be: do you accept that offer of a post-graduate place you had yesterday? It's Tuesday now, you've got until Thursday at 5 p.m. to decide.

Two major issues which you will almost certainly want to deal with are those of career and finance. Devote more time and energy on these now and you'll reap the rewards long term. Socialising may be fun but it won't bring you the best rate of return career-wise, nor will it help you pay off your debts. Building clarity around your future career and life goals will help you strive towards them. Plotting your career and working up the ladder will bring a higher salary, or making progress with your own business will, for example, help you sort out your finances and debts.

Let's follow these two areas in life further.

Do career and financial audits

Table 1.1 demonstrates some questions to ponder.

Doing an audit like this empowers you because you're choosing to address the situation. You're looking at it head on, dealing with known facts rather than assumptions or guesses. You can move forward by creating an action plan and implementing it. With regard to debts, it is better to know what your bottom line is to prevent yourself getting any further into debt. You may have a student debt of £15,000; but how much further are you prepared to allow yourself to build that up before you start paying it back? £20,000? £30,000? It doesn't mean you'll never go for a wild night out with your friends again but it could mean that you look for other ways to have a wild time so that you can control your finances more firmly. Do it jointly with friends in the same boat and work together to deal with it. There are times when we don't like the decisions we have to make, they are uncomfortable and don't fit in well with the lifestyle we want. But discipline never did anyone any harm and can frequently bring unexpected rewards, not least of which is self-respect and an in-built self-belief that you can turn an uncomfortable situation around.

Table 1.1

Career	Finance
What do I want to achieve in life?	*How much do I owe?*
What is important to me?	*Who do I owe it to?*
What do I have to offer the world?	*How much interest am I paying each*
What am I going to do next?	*lender monthly?*
What could I learn to ensure I get to	*What could I do to reduce this inter-*
where I want to be?	*est?*
What are my ambitions and aspira-	*What incomings do I have now?*
tions, dreams and hopes?	*What am I spending it on?*
How far do I want a career which	*What do I have left?*
uses the knowledge I've acquired of	*What could I do to cut back on my*
my subject?	*spending?*
Could I go on to further study?	*How could I pay back my loans and*
Do I need a break?	*debts?*
Where in the world do I want to	*Who could help me?*
work?	*What could I do to get the best deal on*
How far shall I go in my career?	*everything?*
Where can I get constructive,	*What could I do to supplement my*
informed advice (e.g. university	*income?*
careers service, Prospects)?	*When will I start paying everything*
Who do I need to support me?	*back?*
What action(s) will I take to move	*Where can I get constructive, informed*
me closer to where I want to be?	*advice (e.g. bank, building society,*
	student loan company)?
	What action(s) will I take to achieve
	my financical and life goals?

Take action now!

1 List the decisions you need to make now and in the next six months.
2 What have you done so far towards making these decisions?
3 What else do you need to do or to know in order to decide? How will you get that information and where will you get it from?
4 Whose help will you need?
5 When do you need to make each decision?
6 What action will you take?

Many of the decisions in one area of our life will impact on others. For instance, your career choice will affect where you live and work, the structure of your life and the people you work with and/or socialise with. It will impact on your standard of living and your overall happiness. You may need to undertake further training, learning and development to acquire your professional status. Career choice can determine the hours you work and whether you're on call or not, the pace of your working day and your stress levels. The effort you put into your career will affect your ability to pay back your loans and start laying strong financial foundations to your life.

Are you an effective decision maker?

You can learn a lot about yourself from the way you've made past decisions. Take two decisions you've made about your university life or course. Ask yourself:

1   What motivated you to take these decisions?
2   *How* did you make them? For example, was it by gut instinct, by careful research and thought, weighing up the pros and cons, tossing a coin, following the lead of others, force of circumstance or meeting the expectations of others? What process did you follow?
3   Who influenced your decisions and subsequent actions? Who could you have involved more or less?
4   What if anything held you back from making decisions and how did you overcome it?
5   Is a pattern emerging about your decision making? What does it tell you about the way you make decisions? Are there patterns which aren't helping you that you need to break?
6   How can you make your decision making more effective?

In making any decision, there are various factors to take into account as shown in Table 1.2.

Decision-making skills transfer well in life, from making career choices to buying a home. Such skills are essential at work, whether you are self-employed, an employee or the boss, in making business decisions such as the clients you choose to work with, which suppliers you choose to work with and whether you should relocate your business to a more cost-effective area. Action plans to implement our decisions are often interrupted by unexpected obstacles which make the journey more of a roller-coaster ride, but a focus on the end result will help steer us through the rougher patches.

Table 1.2

Possible factors influencing your decision	Choosing modules to study	Choosing your career
Your strengths and skills	What you're naturally good at and wanted to build your skills in	Same for career
Your interests	Following your passions	Same for career – this is what you want to do
What was available?	The modules on offer at your university	What is on offer in the region you work in?
Personal fit	You had a lot of time and respect for the tutor and got on well together; you thought he'd bring out the best in you	You like where the company is going and what it stands for; you met the guys and felt comfortable with them
Long-term plans	You want to go into marketing so this fitted well with your career plans	You choose an employer who can meet your aspirations
How you make decisions	for example '...Ran out of time – just ticked the box for something to do', 'Gut feeling. Everything felt right about this'	for example '...Went for the first thing I saw – can always change later','The moment I walked into the place, I knew it was right for me'

Focus on the result you want and the obstacles will shrink

Often when faced with a decision, we tend to focus too much on possible problems and the negative. *'There are too many graduates...', 'not enough time in the day...', 'I don't want to...'*. Problems have a way of shrinking when put into the context of what we really want. Let's say you get the offer of a dream career from an employer you'd love to work for. The only hitch is that you don't know anyone in the town you'd be living in. It's a totally new area to you. *'Where will I live if I go somewhere new?'* you may ask. But compared to the job offer, which you're wild with excitement about, the accommodation problem is minor. You know you'll sort it somehow. You could lodge for a while as you look. Your new colleagues may know about housing opportunities and good inexpensive places to live. There will be local papers, the HR department may be able to help you or your new boss. You may have friends in the area from university. The most important thing is that you've got the offer you wanted. You found somewhere to live at university; you can do it again.

Have faith in your own ability to create a life for yourself even if you move to a place where you don't know anyone

Yes, it's hard, but you've done it before and survived. You've handled such problems before and you can do so again, thanks to those transferable skills you developed at university, such as the abilities to:

1   start completely afresh – new people, new place, new things to learn, new challenges;
2   take part in and contribute to an organisation – previously, your university, now the workplace, the community, new friends;
3   find your way around and learn the ropes;
4   ask the right questions of the right people to get the answers you need;
5   network and get to know people across the organisation – as you did at university;
6   take the initiative and make things happen – a day at university or college which – lectures and tutorials apart – was pretty much your own;
7   show how adaptable and flexible you are in juggling work, study and social activities, often changing plans at the last minute;
8   organise your time;
9   hunt out new friends and like-minded people you can particularly relate to;
10   relate to people of all different sorts of backgrounds, nationalities and abilities.

University has taught you to think, to question, to be creative, to think laterally, to challenge, to research, to find solutions to problems and to interact. Those skills will never be wasted. And the more you stretch yourself and expand them, the more powerful a resource they will become.

Wait a minute ...

Before you start making decisions, consider what's really important to you.

Where are you going? How does the decision fit into the bigger picture?

A key starting point to making successful decisions involves knowing what is right for you in life or work. You need a strong sense of self-worth and self-awareness. These things encompass areas such as the roles you want to play in life, your career interests, ambitions, aspirations, the environments and conditions you thrive in and learn best in, the things you need around you to make you happy and feel fulfilled and those things that are important to you and what you couldn't do without, i.e. your values. Know what you want, and life has more purpose. You'll move faster because you don't deviate from your route spending time doing things you don't want to do. Many people simply wait for that lucky break to knock on their door. Unfortunately, they have a long wait. You can create your own luck, as Dr Wiseman points out in his excellent book *The Luck Factor* (see Further Reading at the end of this book).

What's important to you?

When you live by your values, you look forward to the start of a new day or week, and you wake up with a happy heart. Life feels right, you feel fulfilled with a strong sense of your own self-worth. Your goals, hopes and aspirations seem easier to strive for because you're at your best as you work towards them. You know you're making the right choices and decisions and moving in the right direction. Similarly, the company which recruits staff with values equal to its own has a good feel about it. The staff are happy, motivated, fulfilled and feel appreciated. They look forward to going to work and are a tight-knit team.

Five signs when life – and work in particular – does not encapsulate your values are:

1   You can't perform properly. You get very tired trying to work at something that doesn't gel with you while pretending that all is well.
2   You're frustrated and short tempered, especially as a new working week looms.

3   It's lonely. Everyone else seems to be on a different wavelength to you.

4   You keep thinking, *There must be more to life than this!* This thought persists over time, making you increasingly frustrated and more angry.

5   You're disappointed in yourself because you know that you should cut your losses and leave, but you can't find the *courage* to do it.

Of course, you may find the perfect match and then something hinders its progression: a technological innovation, a change in the markets, a drop in demand, restructuring, redundancy. Employers understand that it takes time to find the right match, and when reading your CV, they consider your achievements, progression, development, future career plans and the person who lies behind the words on paper and portfolio. But it's your responsibility to find the right career and role.

Table 1.3 gives examples of life and career values. Which ones are important to you to have or be in your life and career to make you truly happy and feel successful?

Having considered which values are important to you, you can build a life and career which incorporates them. For example, if

Table 1.3

Winner	Participant	Contributor
Continuous change	Change where needed	Little change
Security	Stability	Risk
Creativity	Performer	Conformity
Compassion	Fair	Faith
Achiever	Influencer	Supporter
Recognition	Status in community	Appreciated
Success	Work–life balance	Fulfilment
Autonomy	Independence	Managed
Visionary	Implement	Support
Adventure	Spirituality	Pleasure
Driver, creator	Follow the leader	Win–win
Wealth	Rewarded	Feel-good factor
Happiness	Freedom	Other

achievement is very important to you, you could look for careers where results are exceedingly important and measured, such as sales roles.

Select the top eight values which are essential to you from those you've ticked above and create a picture of what they mean to you – don't make any assumptions about them. Get the foundations right. If you think that things such as travel, holidays and a good social life are your values, consider what those things *give you* or *provide you with* and you'll have your real values. Then rank those eight in order. Which one is most important? Which values could you *not* do without? And which are you *not* prepared to compromise on?

Compromising in life will bring more win–wins

At some stage in life, you'll need to compromise. For example, let's say you want to work for an ethical company, but the only position you were offered in six months was from a company which, in your eyes, was unethical, what would you do? Would you refuse to take the job and uphold your values or take the offer up and move on as soon as you could?

What happens now?

In the early years after graduation, most people want to establish themselves by getting a foot on the work and housing ladders. Life may look something like that shown in Figure 1.1.

This scenario will also probably apply to a student who:

- has been sponsored by an employer – the key factor is whether the employer and graduate decide to stay together;
- wants to start his own business;

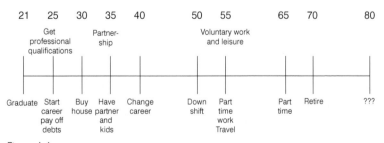

Figure 1.1

 ◆ joins an initiative such as the Knowledge Transfer Partner-
    ship;
 ◆ is a mature student working on his degree with a specific ca-
    reer plan in mind, either with the knowledge and support of
    his employer or aside from the job he is in now as a way to
    change career;
 ◆ as an international student has been sponsored by his govern-
    ment or a company to study in the UK;
 ◆ as an international student now has clear plans what to do and
    returns home – or stays in the UK with a clearly defined plan.

So what about you?

Figure 1.2 gives you questions to ponder and answer.

Many graduates either have no clear idea of what they want to do
after university, so they take whatever comes their way in the first
three to five years after graduation, as shown in Figure 1.3.

This runway to career take-off may be longer and tougher in
terms of getting that lucky break, the opportunity or gap in the

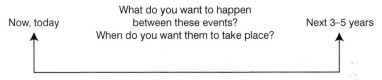

Now, today

What do you want to happen
between these events?
When do you want them to take place?

Next 3–5 years

 • Within five years, working abroad on projects
 • More of a strategic role with the company I'm with now
 • Use my knowledge and expertise to help small companies
   expand overseas
 • Get qualified and moving into management
 • Working in Dubai on development there
 • Qualified as a ...
 • Paid off ...% of my student loans and started to ...
 • Settled down into life after university
 • Found my partner for life

Figure 1.2

Graduates

Starts temping
to pay off
debts and get
experience

Starts applying
for jobs he
wants in the same
area he is now

Lands a job
and needs to
start at the bottom

Career takes
off

Figure 1.3

market, especially as you are probably trying to begin a new life at the same time. You may hook a lower-level job, just to get going, and you'll need a real rocket thrust of persistent effort to get yourself to where you aspire to be. Keep focused on your goal, and you'll head in the right direction. If you lose your focus, your ambitions will take longer to achieve, or they may lose their impetus and fizzle out.

Do you want a job, a career or a business?

These are very different things. Jobs fit well into short-term plans and bring the money in, but they don't necessarily stretch you or pay well. Consequently they can make you feel bored and disillusioned, especially when you weigh up your salary against your student debts. Careers run over a course of time, enabling you to develop your skills, expertise and experience in one particular sector, often climbing a career ladder to reach the upper echelons of the business and sector. You may have a view of the top of this ladder from the bottom or you may create the view, rung by rung, as you climb up. Of course, a job can become a career if you take the initiative, yank it up a gear and get yourself noticed, i.e. take two rungs at once. You could also decide to set up your own business, which enables *you* to make all the decisions: what you will sell, the who, what, when, why, how and where.

By the end of your life, you may have had all of these.

How does your career fit into your life?

You need to find the work–life balance that's right for you, your life and your dependants. At first, this may be hindered as you devote time to establishing yourself and getting a foot on the work and housing ladders, putting bricks and blocks down to get the life you want – the house, family life, network of friends, security, professional qualifications where appropriate, the opportunity for advancement and professional growth, recognition and appreciation. You may prefer to focus on having fun, rather than sorting out your career and life. *Well, there's always next year.*

A hunger for success at work can seriously impact on your quality of life. If your goal was to make your first million within three years after leaving university, and you succeeded, but you lost all your friends in the process because you were always working, would you still deem that a success? Some graduate programmes demand that you dedicate 60, 70, 80 or even 90 per cent of your life to work. You may be prepared to give that early in your career if it takes you to where you really want to be, or you may prefer to opt for a more sensible work–life balance which takes you to a rung on the ladder which you're happy with.

What matters is the *degree of control* we each have over our work–life balance. If you decide to work 100 hours a week to make that first million, that's your choice. Work–life balance becomes an issue when we feel we *don't* have a choice; that other people are making decisions for us about the hours we need to put in. Some employers place a higher priority on work–life balance than others. the most demanding employer may be the person who runs their own business.

As you create a vision of your future career, build specifics into the picture so that you can build plans around them. For example:

* What is your career goal, outcome or end result? If it makes things easier, look at this over a three- to five-year period.
* Why is this important to you?
* How exactly is your career important to you?
* Where do you want to be doing it?
* When are your timescales/deadlines for achieving your goal?
* Who will you be doing it with?
* Who can help you?
* How will you get there? What are the different ways you could reach the outcome you want?
* What can you do to boost your chances of success?
* What can you control? What is outside your control?
* Which deadlines do you need to look out for, such as applying for post-graduate courses, work experience placements and internships?
* What in life and in your career are you *not* prepared to risk, e.g. your integrity, values, standards, expectations of yourself, key relationships ... and what *are* you prepared to risk.

The *why* is important. If you don't understand *why* something is important to you, it is far less likely to happen. If you understand how a goal relates to your values – for example, keeping fit is important to you because you value good health which gives you the freedom to live your life to the full – then you're more likely to achieve it.

Wherever you are, pinpoint careers help available to you

Find out what careers advisory services are available to you where you are *now*, face-to-face, online and by telephone. Sometimes you just need to sit down and talk through your future with someone whom you can trust who is impartial, qualified and trained. Tap into local universities and colleges, your old university and other private agencies in your area for access to careers information and support. Most higher education institutions allow graduates to use their facilities for up to two or three years after graduation and they may also help graduates from any university wishing to move into, remain in or return to their area. You may be charged for some services.

Finally, don't forget that your degree has taught you many transferable skills. Use the forward and strategic planning skills you acquired throughout your degree experience to plan your career and life. Take the initiative and put your brain and energy to work.

Summary action points

Look back at your life overall:

1   How much has it consisted of what you want so far? What efforts have you put in to make sure that happened?
2   What lessons have your past choices taught you as you look to your future?
3   What do you want to achieve *in your life* in the next five years? What would that mean to you?

Chapter 2

Creating your career

Building on your creative and innovative spirit

This chapter is all about helping you to create a vision of what you want your career to consist of. Even if you have a picture, use the self-assessment exercises to add depth to it. Stand back and look at yourself, as if you were looking at the ground from a helicopter, and the distance will help you think more clearly.

Rather than canter laboriously through one career after another, this chapter will pose various questions for you to consider when plotting your life after graduation, so that you can highlight what is important to you.

What are your passions and motivators?

If you want to be happy and successful in your career, get passionate. Find something to do which really inspires and motivates you and stirs you to action, which gives you a real buzz. If you have a real passion for developing people, you could go into training or teaching, but use your talents and skills to bring out the best in people. You may be fascinated by improving systems and processes, or have a passion for solving problems certain groups have in society, perhaps driven by your own life experiences.

Consider the following questions.

- ◆ What excites you and inspires you? What grabs your interest over a sustained period of time?
- ◆ What are you passionate about?
- ◆ What do you want to make a difference to, or particularly do something about?

- How do you want to make a difference to the world, a local community or a group of people?
- What secret dreams and aspirations do you have? How could your degree and life experiences help you to fulfil them?
- What makes you jump out of bed in the morning? What could you work all day at and then plough into the night over?
- What drives your passions and lies behind them? What does your passion give you that nothing else does?

How hungry are you to turn these passions into action?

You may have some passions and interests, causes and aspirations in mind already. How hungry are you to pursue them in your career? Do you want to pursue them that bit further and study them at a post-graduate level or research them? You may have specialised on one or two areas within your degree, or indeed, focused entirely on the subject for the duration. Can you spot a business opportunity which will demand full use of your knowledge, skills and passions? Could you make a living from them, and if so, how? Could you work for someone else with a mutual interest and feeling, or set up on your own, or form a spin-out company from a university, depending on how much you want to focus on it . (A spin-out company is created by a university when research generates a product which is commercially viable.) Are you ravenous to take your passions on board, or just wanting to nibble at them a bit and take on other flavours as well? How fulfilled would you be if you turned them into a career which you worked at 48 weeks of the year and thought about outside working hours? Without that hunger, that ravenous feeling, you're not likely to follow them through and succeed. If you nibble here and snack there, you'll feel less fulfilled, and still feel a longing for something which really hits the spot.

What do you want to contribute to the world?

Have you thought about the contribution you can make to society, your local community, customers, clients and people at large?

- What role do you want to play in changing our landscape and vision?

- What impact do you want your skills and talents and capabilities to have on the world around you?
- Who do you most want to help or work for?
- What do you want to contribute to humanity?
- What sort of sector do you want to be surrounded by and work in?
- Which particular sectors and industries do you want to be closely allied to and work with?

Whether you're into design, construction, engineering, finance, management or planning, they all have a role to play in getting projects and creations off the ground and impacting heavily on the lives of others, be they business clients, victims of a disaster such as an earthquake or tsunami, a community through the building of a new road network or the creation of a new water system in China, or the lives of individuals by biomedical research. Perhaps you want to contribute to the conservation of buildings, or create new facilities for local communities such as schools or hospitals, or major events such as the Olympics, or play a role in the development of countries such as Dubai. And as you know, each sector or group has specific roles within it at different levels of work and their own areas of speciality.

Consider the following questions.

- How do your passions relate to the sectors you are most interested in and their niche areas? Who is working on them and which companies are involved? Which universities have postgraduate courses on them or academic staff researching them? Which are the most relevant research institutes?
- How much do you know about the engineering/construction/design sectors? Are there any areas which excite you but which you don't know much about?

It may be that you have a passion for a particular aspect of your course and chose modules in it but that you don't know a great deal about working in that specialist niche area. Now is the time to find out more by contacting professional bodies and researching careers sites. Consider, too, how you want to use your degree subject.

How do you want to position your career?

Take a look forward, at least for the next five years or so. Where do you see yourself working?

Do you see yourself doing something directly related to your degree or a particular part of your degree?

Such a choice will inevitably involve working for professional status and qualifications with an on-going programme of personal development. The initial rung on the ladder could take four years to strive for but the rewards at the top are fantastic. Such a choice may make full use of the scientific and technical skills you have developed at university and you will need to keep learning and studying them throughout your working life, or at least so long as you work in those sectors. Your job specific knowledge will be core and in use every day as you use the skills you have been taught and learnt at university and apply them to your daily working life and working situations. Table 2.1 shows how extensive the industry is.

Do you want to work as a specialist, on something which particularly excites and interests you?

Ask yourself if there is one or several parts of your degree course which you wish to develop into a career. Can you see yourself doing that day in and out and making a living out of it? Do you enjoy pushing back the boundaries of knowledge and undertaking research, taking an innovative approach? If you can combine that with

Table 2.1

Architecture	Facilities
Building Construction	Financial management
Built environment	Information
Building services	Health and safety
Civil engineering	Land management and surveying
Communications	Manufacturing
Computing	Power
Construction	Structural engineering
Commercial management	Technology
Design	Town planning
Electrical/electronic engineering	Transport

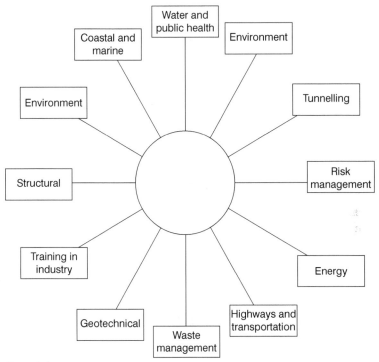

Figure 2.1

an entrepreneurial spirit and apply your new knowledge to markets, you could set up on your own or create a spin-out company working alongside or for a university. You may find yourself working on a particular product or technology, or part of a process or system, such as the initial design or health and safety, for a university department or research institute, or for a research and development department within a company.

Every sector has its own specialisms and you need to dig deep to find out what those are and how they relate to your degree. An example is that of Civil Engineering, as shown in Figure 2.1.

One of these areas may interest you more than others. Which employers cover the areas you're interested in and have something to contribute to? Where can you find out about them?

Within each sector, there will be specialist networks – a great many of them. Many of these are listed at the back of this book, while others can be found via the many engineering and built environment portals. You can check the Internet for companies which specialise in your niche area and find out what they do, who they recruit, their size and what they are working on. You may have focused on them already as part of your degree. Additionally, you can tap into relevant networking groups. Alternatively, would you prefer to transfer some of the skills and knowledge you have acquired to allied industries?

Many sectors are experiencing skill shortages which may mean that it is hard to find people to work in various specialisms. When this happens, good graduates are in high demand, so long as they have the relevant qualifications. Flood Risk Management, for example, has a serious skills shortage – and yet we've all heard a lot about the dangers of flooding and, indeed, seen it first hand, especially with the changing climate.

Don't forget, however, that if you're going to work in the engineering and built environment sectors, you will need key transferable skills such as empathy, the ability to communicate and listen, to solve problems, engage everyone in the process who will be using the end result, and then effectively present ideas.

Do you want to work in a field allied to your degree subject?

This could include working for estate agencies, in the field of health and safety, facilities management, property and building developers, suppliers of services and products to the industry. The knowledge you have acquired during your degree will enhance your effectiveness at work and you will need to keep up-to-date with trends, developments and new products, but you will perhaps not need to head for the heights of professional status. It could involve working as a lecturer or teacher in higher education or becoming a trainer and delivering continued professional development courses and training to employers in the private, public and voluntary sectors.

Enjoyed the degree, but ...

You may feel that a career using the knowledge you've acquired in your degree studies just isn't for you – that it's time to change direction and move away from the subjects you've been studying. The key here is to show potential employers that you have thoroughly thought through your change of heart, and done your research properly. There are plenty of people who have done engineering/construction degrees – and then switched tracks completely. Sometimes, their knowledge provides an advantage in their future careers. It will probably prove helpful in their personal lives. The point is not to follow through your degree because you feel you *should, ought to* or must but because you *want* to. Better to explore thoroughly the reasons for not continuing in your own mind, then move on and focus on what you *do* want to do. Your technical skills and capabilities will give you a different viewpoint to many others competing for the same roles. Have you really, truly explored the world and opportunities open to you if you decide to qualify with professional status?

Do you want to work in a particular business function as opposed to a technical one but nonetheless work for a company in the industry related to your degree?

One option ahead for you is to work for companies but do so by focusing on one of several business functions, such as sales and marketing, finance, human resources, IT, compliance, strategic planning and management, operations and public relations. These all have their own professional bodies and qualifications in their own right and again you will find that you need to keep up-to-date with all the changes in legislation and regulations coming in from your home country, international organisations, professional bodies and customer demands. Working in the industry to which your degree was allied will enable you to understand the technical side of the sector whilst offering your project management skills and abilities in logical thinking, lateral thinking, creativity and team working.

Graduates have a wider choice of careers than ever before. This choice has been increasing in length and breadth over the decades, moving from a range of careers for which a degree was essential, such as teachers, medical sciences and veterinary science, to those areas where, increasingly, employers seek graduates as their first choice. Initially, this hit areas such as management, administrative posts in the public and private sector and IT, but recently degrees have been sought by new sectors. Examples include management accountancy, sales and marketing and buying and purchasing. Many of these have graduate trainee schemes. There are also, increasingly, the back office support roles in operations and compliance, administration and office management. This is especially so as executive assistants and personal assistants increasingly take on the work of junior and middle management.

Getting an idea of what is 'out there'

You may decide to lay your career foundations through a graduate trainee scheme, in which you develop a range of skills and experience as you move around departments, spending a few weeks in each of areas such as HR, IT, marketing, PR and training. Temping can be a route to finding the right place in the workplace for you, and the right role from which to start your career. This is a great way to find your niche and the right company as you move from one to another *and* start paying off those student debts. Portfolio working is another option. For example, working for an employer and setting up your own business as well, perhaps by buying into a franchise, or getting involved with network marketing of starting up your own web company. When you're looking for work, emphasise your transferable skills and the research you've done into the careers you want to enter.

Many graduates moving into work for which a degree is not required, such as retail, bar and restaurant work or lower-level administrative roles, often do so simply to start work, or perhaps in order to save money to go travelling. If you choose to take such a role you will need to try that much harder to pull yourself out of it if you want to change career or progress. Strategic planning can help you work your way out of it, together with regular self-assessment, plotting, planning, monitoring and reviewing while everyone else parties and sleeps.

Over two-thirds of the vacancies advertised in the year up to the end of July 2004 in *Prospects Today* were for graduates of any degree discipline. This means that you have a wide choice of potential careers, such as marketing, finance, human resources, where your ability to come up with ideas and make things look good will be most welcome or working in general management in commerce or industry. This could open up opportunities for you with large corporates of 5,000+ staff. (Here the application process could move to assessment centres, online applications, psychometric testing and more but the thought of that shouldn't put you off, rather it should present a challenge.)

An additional factor to add to the equation is the results you want to achieve at work.

What results do you want to achieve?

You can get a certain idea for where your future lies by considering the results you want to achieve through your efforts. Both affect you motivation to do the job and your happiness in it. Look back over your degree studies and university experiences:

* What were the three most important achievements?
* What did they have in common?
* What results were involved in them?
* How do those results relate to the world of work?
* What results would you like your efforts at work to have most of all?
* Who would you like them to affect most?

What sort of customers or clients do you want to provide a product or service for?

If you decide to go into the business world, then you have a number of choices ahead of you with regards to the employer you choose to work for and those they seek to serve. Your choice can affect your day-to-day work and who you spend much of your working day dealing with. Examples of possibilities include:

1 Business/organisation to business/organisation, perhaps designing a new factory for a car manufacturer or supplying construction products to companies.
2 Business to customer, where you're selling your company's goods to a customer – such as architects would sell their services and expertise to a couple wanting to build an extension to their home.
3 Customer to customer, for example, landscaping a home owner's garden.
4 Public sector or voluntary organisations, or international bodies. For example, working for an education authority as a health and safety officer.

This opens up to you the possibility of working in a huge range of specialist companies, such as architects, building suppliers, the public sector, the computer games industry, exhibition designers, private consulting engineering firms, building and civil engineering

contractors to national and local government, research establish-
ments and education institutions, and industrial organisations.
There may be a few opportunities in the public sector. If you want
to enjoy the opportunity to work abroad, you may need to join a
larger firm which may have offices overseas so that you have the opportunity to join colleagues on different projects.

What role do you want to play?

Within these sectors and companies (depending on their size) you'll
have different levels of careers, attained as people work their way
up the ladder. Some may be relatively unstable, such as project manager and contractors, involving a heavy emphasis on skills such as
pulling projects together so that every aspect of them happens on
time and within budget. Your skills in self-promotion and networking will need to be as finely tuned as those of doing a great job while
you're on a contract. A supervisor may have control of teams working on projects. At the top, a managing director will have a broader
overview of the business as a whole.

The role you aspire to can make a difference to where you position your career and it will be affected by your values. If achievement is important to you, then being a leader, manager or entrepreneur may appeal. If you're a risk taker, then the freelance life will
suit you more than if you prefer the security of being an employee.
Think about the roles you've played in your life in all the teams
you've participated in. Are you a natural leader or do you prefer to
be a supportive player? Do you want to be, for example:

- a company owner
  small or micro-business owner
- a leader
  the boss, team leader, managing director, CEO, chairman
- manager
  project manager, implementing someone's vision
  finance manager, in charge of the budget
- technician
  doing the technical aspects as opposed to strategic and business
  planning
- support, ensuring everything runs smoothly behind the
  scenes
  facilities manager, buildings manager

- entrepreneur
  creating a business out of a vision
- freelance support
  providing a service or product to businesses as and when required
- technical support/advisory desk
  providing a service within an organisation to colleagues or on a business to customer, customer to customer basis
- contractor
  having the freedom to move from one contract to the next, never knowing where each will lead or how long they will last
- researcher
  working to produce new products and services, to innovate

Do you want a career which enables you to take on more and more responsibility so that increasingly you are in charge of the big picture for an entire company, overseeing strategy, mission, vision and goals, rather than taking on responsibility for specific projects for a client? If you're heading down the self-employment and freelance route, how will you handle essential tasks such as agreeing and signing contracts, dealing with health and safety, balancing the books, product and business development, planning your vision and goals for the business, tax, insurance and handling staff?

Going it alone or in a small team

What will life be like working for a small company or being the boss of one?

Small companies have many advantages: you'll probably enjoy more varied responsibilities and see the entire design or artistic process from start to finish, being involved at every stage. You'll have a finger on the pulse and know what's happening and you'll need to be resilient and pro-active in developing your career and seeking the training you need. The work environment will be less structured and hierarchical, and the decision-making processes faster.

There is, of course, a flip side, either to running your own business or working for a small business. Put yourself in the shoes of the company owners as *business* people. They've probably put a huge amount of time and money into their company, yet they still go through peaks and troughs of work. One week, they will be working flat out, while the next they will be gloomily wondering where the next piece of business will come from. They will need more staff for peak busy periods, and very few in others and that need can change from one hour to the next. The bosses probably spend too much time and energy and focus on the 'doing', rather than devoting them to strategic planning and business development. Many bosses are being strangled by legislation such as health and safety and employment laws. Every time he or she takes on a new employee, they worry whether the new member of staff will disappear on maternity or paternity leave or fit in with the rest of the team. Will there be sufficient work long term to justify another member of staff? Visit any of small business networking sites and you'll quickly get a feel for the issues concerning them. They will prepare you for what lies ahead and the working culture you may find.

What skills do you want to use, i.e. what do you want to do all day?

This can be particularly useful if you would like to change career altogether and move away from engineering and the built environment; but even so, the exercise will help you pinpoint your strengths and skills you particularly want to use at work.

- Look back over your life experience to achievements you particularly enjoyed. What were you doing when you did them?
- What skills do you particularly enjoy using now?
- What skills would you like to feature strongly in your career? (You don't need to stick to those you know – you can learn new skills.)
- What knowledge do you want to work with in your career? Start to pinpoint the products and services you want to work with.

Table 2.2 gives plenty of examples of skills.

The next stage is to consider what areas of work use the skills you've highlighted. In what capacity do you wish to use the skills you've acquired through your degree studies? Look back through your course and pinpoint them. How could you link them all together in a career? What would the picture look like if you were using such skills in your career?

Table 2.2

Accounting	Evaluating	Producing
Achieving	Finding solutions	Product design and
Acquiring	Fundraising	manufacturing
Administering	Guiding	Programming
Advising	Helping	Project management
Analysing, e.g.	Identifying	Promoting
problems	Implementing	Qualitative skills
Answering	Influencing	Quantitative skills
Applying	Innovating	Questioning
Assembling	Inspiring	Recommending
Assessing	Interviewing	Researching
Building	Inventing	Researching and
Business analysis	Investigating	developing
Buying	Keeping records	Securing
Caring	Learning	Selecting
Challenging	Liaising	Selling
Classifying	Listening	Servicing
Coaching	Locating	Setting targets
Cold calling	Making	Sketching
Communicating	Managing	Strategic management
Computer application	Marketing	Strategic planning
Conducting discussions	Measuring	Studying
Conserving	Mentoring	Summarising
Consulting	Monitoring	Supervising
Counselling	Motivating	Supporting
Creating	Negotiating	Taking risks
Critical thinking	Networking	Talking
Dealing	Numeracy	Teaching
Debating	Operating	Teamworking
Designing	Organising	Training
Detecting, e.g. false	Persuading	Understanding
logic	Planning	Watching
Developing	Preparing	Winning
Diagnosing	Presenting	Working alone
Displaying	Pricing	Working with others
Distributing	Problem solving	Writing
Driving concept into	Processing	Other
real product		

You could apply any of these skills to a career within a larger company where your degree knowledge is useful; for example, working in sales and marketing for a construction company. This means that you could move into a number of business function roles, such as compliance, human resources, sales and marketing, finance, IT and office support systems.

Table 2.3

Money, budgets	*Laws/regulations*
General management	Health and safety
Finance	Compliance
Accountancy	Company secretary
Banks, building societies	Human Resources
Financial advisers	
People	*Ideas*
Training and Development	Product development
Human Resources	Design and creativity
Recruitment	Advertising
Teaching	Business development
Lecturing	Innovation
Training/coaching	Enterprise
Targets	*Products, technical expertise*
Recruitment	Marketing
Sales	Research and development
Customer service	Distributing
	Buyer
Processes	*Buildings*
Product development	Facilities management
Disaster management	Health and safety
Distribution manager	Operations management
Events/Conferences/Exhibitions	*Words/language*
Selling	Journalism
Organising	Publishing
Advertising	Technical author
Services	
Marketing	
Customer service	
Insurance	
Building surveyor	

What do you want to apply these skills to? Table 2.3 gives some ideas.

Do you want a career in research?

Do you want to further your knowledge and research skills? There are currently over 20,000 people engaged in research in the UK alone. Many work on a project full time, or combine research with other responsibilities such as lecturing or clinical practice, often with others in the UK or abroad. Researchers are also often employed by research councils, the government, and other relevant organisations to fulfil various responsibilities such as management, policy advice and project planning. As well as considering the usual academic routes, find out what bodies such as Regional Development Agencies (www.englandsrdas.com) are doing in your sector to support the movement of knowledge and ideas out of their scholarly world and into industry and commerce through the commercialisation of research into spin-out companies. (A spin-out company is created by a university when research generates a product which is commercially viable.) These agencies may be targeting specific industries or 'cluster groups' which they see as having particularly strong potential for economic growth in their region.

The Research Assessment exercise means that the higher education funding bodies can distribute funds for research on quality. Find out more by visiting www.rae.ac.uk for information on the Research Assessment Exercise 2008; and www.hero.ac.uk/rae for the 2001 results. Ratings range from 1 to 5* and it gives an idea of the standard of UK research. See Further Reading and Useful Addresses at the end of this book. The normal route into research is to undertake a post-graduate course (see Chapter 3 for more information).

A site which will inspire you if you want to climb the academic ladder is that of the Engineering Professors' Council (www.engprofc. ac.uk/) which represents senior academics from all branches of engineering and which provides a forum for discussion among them. You can find out what the hot topics are of the day. You may also find the Higher Education Academy (Engineering Subject) of interest at www.engsc.ac.uk/, along with the European Society for Engineering Education (www.ntb.ch/sefi/). The Royal Academy of Engineering has awards and schemes designed to encourage research and to strengthen the relationship between academic life and the industrial world, plus industrial secondments, international travel grants and teaching fellowships. Visit also www.innovationandresearchfocus. org.uk which seeks to promote the application of research in building and civil engineering – it seeks to disseminate research news widely and fast.

What's of key importance to you in the career you may choose?

Regardless of the careers you have in mind right now, identify the elements of work which are key to you in your future, such as shown in Table 2.4.

Some sectors in the workplace carry particularly unsociable working conditions which go with the territory. In the creative industries, pay is a bit below other sectors and many opportunities are on a freelance, part-time or short-term basis, so you need to develop strong self-promotion and networking skills, and ensure that your skills are updated regularly so that you can use the latest technology.

Moving your self-awareness forward

Once you've started to identify what's important to you, you can start really focusing on how that relates to the different sectors and opportunities in the workplace.

You can find more careers information about this sector in sites such as:

* The Engineering and Technology Board www.etechb.co.uk. This is a charity seeking to promote the perception of engineering and technology in the UK. It works in partnership with government, industry and business, the professions and the education sector. This drive is to ensure that the UK has the skilled engineers it needs in the future. It produces a survey every other year of registered engineers, covering subjects such as income, means of employment (i.e. self-employed, an employee, contract worker etc.) and how important professional membership, etc. is to respondents.
* www.bconstructive.co.uk has lots of information about careers in the industry.
* Two that should definitely be visited are www.scenta.co.uk/careers and www.enginuity.org.uk.
* Visit too www.careersfair.com/ – an excellent resource with international links in a large number of careers through to many countries, giving details of events and shows, qualifications, careers and training. Not, however, graduate specific.

Once you have started to work out where you want to be and what you want to be doing, create your own goal, desired result – whatever you choose to call it.

You're far more likely to achieve what you want if it is personal to you, reflects your values and excites you. Create a clear picture of what life will be like when you achieve it. Write your goal down as specifically as you can, to help you focus, and put it somewhere you can see it every day. Talk about what you do want to do – as opposed to what you don't – as if it were already happening. Bring your vision alive and infuse it with energy and drive. Give it a time limit, so that you have something to work for. Finally, make it sufficiently challenging to stretch you, but realistic. It will be more manageable if you break it down into bits, and work through it step by step.

An example of a long-term career goal is:

In 5 years' time, I will:
➢ have got my professional qualifications;
➢ have paid off my student debts;
➢ have a network of friends in London I feel I know really well;
➢ be working abroad.

In six months' time, I'll have:
➢ researched all the firms I want to apply to;
➢ signed up with a recruitment company which specialises in …;
➢ made the necessary networking contacts;
➢ attended my first job interview.

A word on family expectations

Families can play a key role in our future career planning, unfortunately sometimes to the detriment of our own judgement of what is right for us. *'I went into it to please my parents'*, often means that graduates went into safe, respectable careers which met with nods of approval and sighs of relief from their family, but made them, the graduate, feel they were en route to jail for a working lifetime. Today, most families are more relaxed about career choice – *'You can't tell them – they make their own minds up!'* frequently with all the inference that they still know better. They want us to be safe, protected, happy and successful and a misunderstanding of the job market and a tendency to take on board negative messages from the media makes things worse. There's nothing like the unknown and misunderstood to make people select the safe and known. While our friends and family have our interests very much at heart, their own agendas and self-interest may colour their well-meaning advice to us. They know our qualities well, but may have a limited experience and knowledge of the job market. Pinpoint ways to ask for their help, *'It would really help me if you could...'* and suggest a couple of practical ways they could help. And keep your sights high.

Summary action points

Bringing all the answers to the exercises in this chapter together.

1   What sort of a picture of your future career is emerging? What am I doing in it?
2   What information do I need to firm this picture up?
3   What do I need to happen next to help me further my career plans?
4   What do I need to know to start making decisions?

Chapter 3

Working out 'how to'

This chapter is all about the 'how'.

How will you get to where you want to be? What could you do to reach the outcome you want? What will you do to position yourself to be in a strong position to make the life you want happen?

If you take the time-line for a professional graduate career, it may look similar to that shown in Figure 3.1.

Figure 3.2 looks at these questions.

Once you've created your career goal, there are five more stages to work through to achieve it, as shown in Figure 3.3 and outlined on pages 35–7.

Questions to ask yourself as you make the bridge include: what will employers be looking for from someone like me who is just starting out? Answers could be: strong career planning (i.e. even if you're not sure of what it is you want to do, you know what steps

Graduate career   Acquire professional exams and status   Progression

Figure 3.1

Now, today   What do you want to happen between these events? When do you want them to take place?   Next 3–5 years

Create your career goal.
Give it vision and focus.
Then nurture it until you achieve it.
Then set your next one.

Figure 3.2

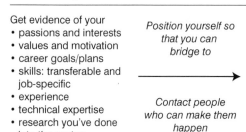

Get evidence of your
- passions and interests
- values and motivation
- career goals/plans
- skills: transferable and job-specific
- experience
- technical expertise
- research you've done into the sector

Position yourself so that you can bridge to

Places where you can apply these things
- employment
- work experience
- internships
- further study
- initiatives such as Knowledge Transfer Partnerships
- post-graduate courses
- short training courses

Contact people who can make them happen

Figure 3.3

you need to take to find out and where you are in that process); a professional approach; desire to achieve and focus on the matter in hand; respect for the world they live in and where they've got to in it; specific questions prepared; enthusiasm; interest; motivation; and a get-up-and-go attitude.

You will also need an understanding of what is required of you from employers. There are three different levels of requirement.

1   Technical experience, knowledge and understanding, and skills for the level of work you are doing and working towards that to which you aspire; showing that you can master the knowledge and analytical skills required for your specialist role.
2   Business acumen and organisation and commercial awareness; understanding how businesses and organisations work and how business functions contribute towards the overall effort.
3   Personal skills, such as leadership, management, the ability to form fast working relationships with people.

You can apply the following five stages at any time in your career, and it is a wise move to apply a review of where you are now and where you want to be regularly and certainly to involve it in your appraisal at work with your line-manager and boss, and an independent one for You Plc at home. In time, as you take on responsibility for other staff members, you can use the five stages to help them develop and plan and progress their careers and reap the rewards of watching others grow and develop. They will help ensure that you attain the future you want and put you firmly in charge of the process. You own it and can plan it in your own time.

The engineering, technology and built environment sectors are, in the broadest sense, continually facing the challenges of increasing customer and client expectations. In addition, there are more rules, regulations, EU and national legislation, technological change and an increasingly competitive world. It is as well to be in fighting shape (mentally, physically and technically) if you are to meet these challenges and rise to them from a position of strength.

Let's consider the five stages which will help you plan and develop your career.

(1) What do you need to do to achieve your career goals?

This involves understanding exactly what you need to do to achieve your goal and be clear about how you will know when you have done so. What measure(s) of success will you use? Research to find out what you need to do will invariably involve talking to some of the following people.

* Employers – what recruits do they need, what are they looking for and how can they help you achieve both your goal and ensure you contribute to theirs?
* Professional bodies and trade associations – so that you clearly understand what is involved in any qualifying process.
* Young professionals who are already making their way up the career ladder you want to climb.
* Your tutors so that you can make sure you are on course for the degree qualification you want.
* Some degree of flexibility is never a bad thing – it could make the difference between getting your foot on the ladder or not.

(2) How far have you got in attaining your goal? What have you done to work towards it?

Be clear about the bank of skills, knowledge and technical expertise you are building up through your degree studies and university life. You can seek evidence of these through:

* work experience, paid and unpaid;
* voluntary work;
* travel;

- your degree studies thus far;
- any professional exemptions you have accrued.

Once you've got your evidence, you can bridge it to potential employers' needs and your own potential and top performance.

(3) What have you done to position yourself to boost your chances of success in achieving your goal?

This may involve activities such as:

- work experience relevant to your career;
- undertaking an internship or work experience scheme;
- studying for a post-graduate qualification to give you that specialist knowledge;
- working for an accredited degree;
- joining the student branch of your professional organisation;
- attending professional meetings, campus presentations and careers fairs;
- focusing on what you want and committing energy and time to ensuring that you achieve it.

(4) What else do you need to do to attain your career goal, be it short, medium or long term?

Figure 3.4 shows the possible next steps you could take.

These steps may *all* feature at some time in your working life, alone or in combination. They may just appear as an opportunity too good to miss. Right now, you may feel like a complete break from academia and work, and head off for six months' break. And if you are planning on remaining in the sector or heading or professional and management status, acquiring professional qualifications and status will almost certainly feature.

(5) How are you progressing on your journey to achieve your goal?

There are a number of things you need to do to achieve your goal.

Figure 3.4

Create an action plan with deadlines and timescales

Within the scope of this timetable, you will need to include activities such as:

- researching your options – possible routes to where you want to be;
- meeting people and networking in the right places;
- preparing applications and sending them off;
- researching the companies in your sector;
- attending careers fairs, presentations, interviews – get the dates from university careers services in advance and any other sources you can find;
- updating your CV and any information you have about yourself online (and stay clear of blogs).

Create a clear vision

One of the first things you need is a vision, especially if you're setting up your own business. Imaging filming yourself on video at work immediately after university, then wind the film forward to three to five years' time. Where are you and what are you doing? Your answers will help you plot your path to success by breaking the longer period down into manageable chunks and then tackle them one by one. That way, it's easier to focus on where you're headed.

Give your career the prominence in your life and the attention it deserves

Focus your energies in the right direction with a plan. It will fill your life with purpose and energy, and you'll waste less time on things which aren't important. You can consider all the different ways to get to where you want to be, and to position yourself to take the best route to make it happen.

Time management and the ability to change focus will be essential if you want to work on a full or part-time basis while building your portfolio and establishing yourself.

You need to discipline yourself and be swift to adapt from the day job to your real passion, and not waste any time slumping in front of the television for a 30-minute break which can then last the entire evening. A sharp 30–40 minutes' exercise, meditation or yoga can do wonders for clearing your mind and re-energising your mind, soul and body as you switch from one job to the other. Find a pattern which works for you. If you work well in the morning, do a couple of hours while the rest of the country sleeps and then go out to the day job knowing you've already made headway in your real job. It makes you feel positive.

Undertake a skills audit

What further skills do you need to make the leap from where you are now to where you want to be? This could be in areas such as interview technique, practising for assessment centres or CV writing. Alternatively, if you want to run your own business, it could be in subjects such as business functions, customer care, marketing and selling, health and safety issues, branding and motivating people. What steps can you take to really ensure your skills are top notch? What training do you need? This may or may not be sector specific.

Enrolling for professional qualifications

You may plan to study for professional qualifications once you have decided on the business function you wish to work with. These qualifications give you the core knowledge and competences which you need to perform effectively at work; they give you the theory and practice which gives you a competitive edge. In some industries, you cannot advise clients or practice without them. Working towards them normally involves taking a number of examinations and practical experience. Consider which is best for you (talk about this with your employer, but do some fact finding about professional qualifications as you move through your career decision-making process). Think about how you want to study, be it online, by evening class, through block learning or distance learning. Professional bodies will have a list of accredited training providers and most have a very considerable range of support mechanisms to help you through.

Be sure about what you need to do to attain the (professional) status you want

Let's take engineering as an example. The Engineering Council (www.engc.org.uk) sets and maintains the standards of professional competence and ethics for engineers, technologists and technicians. It runs the Register of Chartered Engineers, Incorporated Engineers and Engineering Technicians.

Find out about what you need to do to gain your professional qualifications and status. This may involve:

1   enrolling as a graduate student member of the right professional body.
2   gaining experience as part of a project team under the supervision of an experienced professional;
3   undertaking the chartership process with the aim of becoming a chartered engineer;
4   achieving charter status;
5   progressing over time to become, e.g., a senior structural engineer or project engineer.

The Engineering Council (ECUK) has a directory of UK engineering institutions at http://www.engc.org.uk/Institutions/Institutions. aspx and FEANI (European Federation of National Engineering Associations) also has an index on its website at www.feani.org. You can find out about the registration process at www.engc.org.uk/ Registration/Registration_Process.aspx. Finally, visit www.pd-how2. org/ which is the site of the Professional Development Partnership, made up of professional development teams from IMECHE, the Institution of Engineering and Technolgoy, IOP and RAeS.

Heading up the career ladder to chartered status – or do you go for incorporated?

Do you want a graduate training scheme with a planned career development leading to Chartered Engineer or Incorporated Engineer status? Find out the answers to the following questions.

+ What is the difference and what impact will that have on your proposed career development?
+ What is involved in its study and how does that make you feel after three or four years of study?
+ How does each fit into your long-term career plans and how are they viewed outside the sectors by employers, e.g. if you wanted a career change and to move up the career ladder?

'My degree wasn't accredited by the relevant professional organisation'

Get in touch with your professional body with details of your university, the degree title and discipline, level of award and mode of study (i.e. part or full time, etc.), whether or not it was a sandwich course and the dates you studied for it. Most professional bodies have a list of accredited degrees on their sites.

Should you transfer from a BEng to an MEng?

The MEng enables you to progress rapidly into a position of leadership and, consequently, the final two years include professional engineering, business and management content. You can transfer from BEng to MEng. Find out by talking to professionals in your intended specialist area how the two are viewed amongst professionals, and then identify which is the most appropriate for you in the long term.

As you look for work, take into account potential employer's experience in taking people through professional qualifications

Find out what mechanisms potential employers have in place to help you through your career progression, such as appraisals, accredited training schemes, competence frameworks and informal training and links with professional bodies and colleges to ensure that their employees are trained, skilled, up-to-date and qualified. If an employer is relatively new to all this, find out how open they are to having support from professional bodies to help them through the process.

What further learning do you need to undertake to get to where you want to be?

There are various forms of learning: informal, where you find the information you need to mug up on and learn about it yourself; and the more formal, set in short or longer courses. Identify what you need to know or have expertise in to be successful in the work you want to do, find out where you can get this learning and what you need to apply for it (resources, financial, knowledge, talent etc.) and then do it. One of the first ideas which may occur to you is that of doing a post-graduate degree.

To be ... a post-graduate or not?

If you want to specialise further following from your under-graduate degree, you could do a post-graduate course. It's vital to be passionate about your subject at these academic heights.

Post-graduate courses come in different guises. Some involve an element of teaching and research and some are straight research. In some industries, a post-graduate qualification can really benefit you in terms of springing into a career area. Courses may be designed to enhance and deepen your knowledge in a particular area, such as lighting design or building conservation; or to act as a springboard into an area of employment, such as land surveying, or a specific business function area, such as management, marketing, human resources or banking. Alternatively, you could enrol for research-based studies, such as a PhD (Doctor of Philosophy).

Some employers sponsor employees through degree and post-graduate courses and may even approach a university to create a bespoke course and qualification for their employees. Equally, some people study a post-graduate degree for their own (career) development, perhaps part time or online. People study post-graduate degrees for various reasons, to boost their career prospects or to simply increase their specialist knowledge and expertise in a particular area. Many students work for several years before taking a full-time post-graduate degree. By this time, they can envisage exactly how that study will fit into longer-term career plans, plus they've got experience to talk about when they finally come to getting that post-graduate job. Timing is tricky – leave it too long and it may be too late to put impetus and fresh energy into your career.

Questions to consider before you sign up for a post-graduate degree

1   How does this course take you closer to achieving your long-term career plans? Where does it fit within them?
2   Will a post-graduate degree substantially boost your chances of success? Will it really give you that edge over your competitors? What do employers think?
3   Are you contemplating post-graduate study simply to put off joining the working world for another year? (The longer you leave it, the harder it may be.)
4   What are the costs and what funding is available?
5   What have post-graduate students gone on to do after their studies? How do these paths relate to your aspirations?
6   What will it take to be a successful applicant and student?
7   What are your true motivations for taking such a course (e.g. entry into a new career, career progression)?
8   Is it really a post-graduate course you need, or would another form of study and learning be more appropriate for the skills and knowledge you seek? Get specific about your learning needs.
9   What evidence do you have that post-graduate study will enhance your employment prospects? Could networking and getting the right experience under your belt, perhaps by doing an internship, be as effective? Weigh up your options and talk to professionals in the field before you decide what to do. Consider, too, where you want to work. Some countries place greater emphasis on work experience than qualifications, others will be the opposite.

Further information on post-graduate studies

You'll find the official UK post-graduate database at www.prospects.ac.uk which lists the different courses available by subject, region and institution in the UK. It gives research specialisms, RAE ratings, number of students, duration of course, contact details and, importantly, the programme aims, including the level of importance in areas such as vocational/occupational training, professional development, research and scholarship, and preparation for research. It is worth noting that an increased number of post-graduate courses can be studied online or part-time. You can apply online through Prospects, and even use some sections of the application for different courses which will save you time. In the UK, apply as soon as you can because the more popular courses fill up quickly – this means often October or November in the year before the course is due to start. The National Postgraduate Committee (www.npc.org. uk) represents the interests of post-graduate students in the UK.

If you live outside the UK, the British Council (www.britcoun. org) has offices throughout the world and can give you lots of information about studying and living in Britain. The National Academic Recognition Information Centre (NARIC, www.naric.org.uk) provides a service for international students who want information on the comparability between international and UK qualifications.

Short courses may be just the ticket

A short course may boost your employability and give you the skills you need to get that post you want or the knowledge you need to make a specific move happen. In the UK, you can find these at www.hotcourses.com: find out too what local college and private training companies have to offer. Courses relating to the workplace should include a stint of work experience to give you confidence and practice, and the course tutors should also have strong contacts with employers in the sector. When you have pinpointed what you want to do then, if you are lacking any particular skills, a short course could be just the ticket to close the gap between what you've got and what employers want. A career development loan (www. direct.gov.uk/cdl) may be last thing you feel like acquiring but if you live in the EU, it could provide you with the finance you need to fill that vocational skill gap and boost your employability. Some professional bodies provide workshops on how to qualify as a professional; the tax office offers workshops on being self-employed if you're inclined to take that route.

Consider flexible learning

Don't restrict your learning to being in the classroom. You can learn through your own informal reading, conferences, events, seminars, workshops, exhibitions, fairs, network meetings, online forums, articles, books and more.

Short on skills and business knowledge?

A combination of subjects taken at university may have given you skills and knowledge in areas such as business studies, administration, marketing and public relations. You may need to pick these up through short courses on offer locally. LearnDirect (www.learndirect.co.uk) offers such courses to small companies. ACAS (www.acas.org.uk) offers a small number of courses on employment law at a very cost-effective rate.

Continually review your progress

You need to do this every four to six months in the early stages of your career and then six to 12 months later to ascertain your career and development are moving in the direction you want them to go and take action if this is not the case. Enlist the help of mentors, coaches, careers advisers, professional bodies, friends and your employer to help you. If you are not making the progress you want, pinpoint why. It may be that you are not devoting the time you need to undertake your studies and some attention to your time and energy management skills is required. Perhaps you need exposure to different projects at work or university to get the experience you need.

Congratulate yourself as you progress!

And then review and revise your career plans and goals, and start the five stages all over again.

You may, of course, be working already

If you studied part time while working, look back to the reasons why you enrolled for an under-graduate or post-graduate degree. Perhaps you did so with your employer's knowledge, blessing and support. If this is the case, discuss your future with your employer, your direct boss or HR or both. Questions to ask include:

* What do I want to happen next?
* Where do I see my career going in the next five years?
* How do I see myself doing this: with my current employer, with another employer or starting up alone?
* What do I need to do now to make this happen?
* How has my new degree status changed my CV and what I have to offer?

Re-write your CV for your next perfect role, or write a job description for the role you really crave. What is missing from where you are now and where you want to be? Perhaps it's taking on a new project which will give you exposure to a particular experience or new skillset. You may feel that your current company cannot fulfil you career aspiriations, but ensure there are no other options open to you with them first. Talk to your line-manager and HR department about the studies you've been doing and find out how the company can best use them. If you don't use them, you'll waste them.

Outside of the office, ask yourself if your current employer can help you meet your career aspirations. Your goals may have changed since you started the course; you may want to change career or go it alone, or start afresh with another company. If your employer sponsored you through your degree, did you commit to staying with the company for a given length of time after graduating? If you did, you may need to negotiate an exit.

Whatever you choose to do, stretch your new confidence and intellectual prowess. Work to achieve your potential, not to reduce it because your current role isn't right for you. That may mean cutting the strings with your current employer.

Planning to go it alone?

Running your own business is about fulfilling your own dreams and not those of someone else. For many, working for someone else deadens their creativity, freedom, independence, fun, being able to work when you want at what you want. There is considerable help for start-ups, from innovative centres where you can hire an office and share facilities at inexpensive rates, to advice from business advisers, events and online sites designed to help you make all the right decisions. Take advice: networking clubs can help you talk to fellow entrepreneurs and to help each other. In September 2004, Chancellor Gordon Brown launched the National Council for Graduate Entrepreneurship (www.ncge.org.uk). It in turn has set up Flying Start (www.flyingstart-ncge.com) and backed by One NorthEast, the area's regional development agency. You could come up with an idea for a product to sell or become a freelance, taking on contract work and charging your services out at an hourly or daily rate to companies.

You could buy a franchise, which is a tried and tested product or set up a business selling products. The British Franchise Association (see Useful Addresses at the end of this book) is the only independent accreditation body for franchising in the UK. Franchises cover a wide range of areas from pet care to refill printer cartridges, art suppliers to training centres. There are also workshops and seminars to give you lots of advice and tips on choosing a franchise and running a successful business. Before you buy any franchise, check its financial status and insist on seeing the accounts from its head office. The website www.careersfair.com also has details of links to franchises in Italy, France, the USA, Canada, Australia and New Zealand, to name a few.

Self-employment is not the rosy picture it often appears. Many small companies are being increasingly strangled by red tape and the compensation culture, and it can be a very lonely affair. Consider how you'll handle tasks such as planning a vision for your business, writing a business plan, setting yourself financial targets, dealing with health and safety issues, accounting and financial responsibilities, taking on staff and keeping to the right side of the law, keeping the books and records, on-going business development, product and service development, dealing with the taxman, accountant and suppliers. There are lots of short courses designed to help you handle this, many run by business advisory services.

Consider the following questions:

+ What do you want your business to achieve? What do you want it to do?
+ What will it look like in five years' time?
+ What financial targets will it meet in six months', one year, three years and five years?

- Who will your customers/clients be? Where will they come from?
- What will your unique selling points be?
- What position will you take in the market?
- What brand do you want? What values will your business portray?
- What will your reputation be based on?
- What message and language can you use to grab potential customers' attention?
- What story would a SWOT analysis give you? (A SWOT analysis looks at the Strengths, Weaknesses, Opporutnities and Threats facing a business.) How does that compare with your competitors in the market?
- What can you do to give your product or service that extra special added value, or to please and surprise your customer or client?
- Where will you run the business from?
- How will running a business impact on your lifestyle?

There will also be key operational questions to ask such as:

- What funding do you need right now to set up and give yourself an income?
- How will you structure the business (e.g. limited company, sole trader, partnership)?
- How will you market your products and services?
- How will you price them?
- What equipment will you need to get started?
- How soon can you get up and running?

If you can't answer these questions, remember that university has given you the ability *to find the answers*. When you started university, you asked where things were, who you needed to talk to in order to get a, b and c done. You knew nothing about the place when you started but you quickly learnt the ropes and found out what you needed to know to make the most of your university days. You can do this again.

Working while developing your own business

Many would-be entrepreneurs take any job going to bring in money while they are working to build up their own businesses. Herein lies a dilemma. It is not uncommon for people to have two or even three jobs at the same time. Many workers in the UK moonlight, doing their bread-and-butter job in the day, and selling merchandise or key skills over the Internet or phone at night. In many cases, these efforts will become full-time businesses. There is the opportunity to work at one thing while looking to achieve a long-term goal doing something totally different. This means that an individual has a divided loyalty which can create stresses and strains, as you change from one culture and role in your paid employment and then come through your front door and switch over to your own special aspirations, goals and the reality of making them work for you.

Time out for golden sands, sea, sun ...

If you've been on the academic treadmill all your life without a break, you may feel like it's time for some time out, fun and rest. Increasing numbers of people all ages are taking time out and more (larger) employers are offering employees sabbaticals. They like seeing them return to the workplace refreshed, with a new confidence, fresh ideas, great soft skills and creativity. Gap programmes too are waking up to the fact that more of us want time out, and providing excellent opportunities for voluntary work and travel. But do a reality check – do you just need a good break and a rest for a couple of weeks, or do you have real, specific motivations for taking time out?

That said, you live your life once. The moment you stop experiencing such adventures as travel and facing challenges in life, you stop living and start existing. Travelling will give you lots of opportunities to collect new ideas and influences, which you can incorporate into your work when you return home. If you plan to take some time out, you could look for a job before you go and try to negotiate a start date for when you return (assuming you will return); or you could travel and look for a job when you get back. This gives you more flexibility and possibly more stress as you wonder how on earth you're going to find a job and pay off your debts as you get home. One possibility is to consider overseas internships and training schemes. See Further Reading at end of this book.

Unemployment ...

Not a very inspiring option, is it? So get busy.

Seven ways to pass the time while you're unemployed

1 Get relevant work experience, even if it's just for a week or a couple of days a week over a month or so.
2 Do voluntary work.
3 Learn new skills.
4 Travel.
5 Job hunt persistently and seriously.
6 Do something quite mad and quirky to make your CV stand out.
7 Study for a qualification which will give you on-the-job skills.

Acknowledge that this is a difficult time, because you've been through all the hard work towards your graduation, celebrated in style, promised complete strangers you met in the Union Bar in the last 24 hours at university that you'll keep in touch ... and suddenly it's all over. And it's a strange feeling, so acknowledge it and then turn your attention to the future.

If your family are helping you in the wrong way, be patient. They simply want to help you and their hearts are in the right place. Show them how they can help you by saying '*What would really help me is if you could...*'. It could be they could introduce you to someone whom you need to talk to about a career move into a specific industry.

Give your life a turbo-boost!

If you're currently sitting at home aimlessly with no defined plans or goals and no meaningful way to fill your day, it's time to change that. We all need to feel appreciated – it's a basic human need. Change the way you're spending your time and energy. If you're joining an industry in which contract and freelance work features heavily, you will need to become accustomed to periods of employment between commissions and contracts and develop strong skills in networking and promoting yourself and your talents.

Start climbing out of where you are now and start walking purposefully to where you want to be.

1   Brainstorm strategies you can use which will boost your chances of success, such as a willingness to move and live where the sector is strongest geographically. If you want to stay where you are, where the sector may be weak or even non-existent, be more flexible in terms of the sort of work you go for.
2   Talk to fellow graduates. What sort of business could you start up together based on your mutual interests and passions?
3   Talk to as many people as you can by going to where you know you'll find them, outside the usual graduate arena, such as trade exhibitions and local networking events.
4   Set yourself daily targets and goals in every area of your life, not just your career. Life isn't just about work.

Summary action points

Move your thinking forward:

1   Which university or college runs the course in the subject I'm looking for?
2   What funding is available for me to set up my own business?
3   What initiatives are available that might be relevant to me and my career goals?
4   What do I need more of in my life? How can I get it?
5   What steps will I take next and how will they move me closer to my goals? What do I need to do to make them happen?

Chapter 4

Connecting with your network

The world's a network

Connecting to those in the know who can help you move closer to the things you want in life will enable you to enjoy a far richer life and career. Chapters 4 and 5 will help you pinpoint people who can help you create or open doors to new opportunities.

A strong, active network can open doors to decision makers and in turn enable you to reach out, help others and live a highly successful and fulfilling life. Whatever stage of life and career you are at, it will enhance your prospects of obtaining the introductions you need. Highly successful people have a network of business associates, acquaintances, colleagues and friends they can turn to for information, advice, introductions and help. You create your own luck and networks in life, however, and they are as active and useful and productive as you make them. Remember that networking is also about helping those who *have* helped you, and those who *haven't*.

This chapter considers the *Who* question in a networking capacity.

+ *Who* can help me?
+ *Who* can give me the support I need now?
+ *Which* websites will be most useful?

Eight steps to successful networking

1   An ability to chat and be really interested in the other person; you need to be able to establish rapport with strangers quickly.
2   Listening and questioning skills.
3   A get-up-and-go attitude – go out there and fight for your place in the world.

4   Follow through. Use the information you acquire, file it for future thought, action it or dump it, but *do* something with it.
5   Lateral thinking – does your contact know of anyone else you should talk to?
6   Respect! The person you're talking to has got to where they are by hard work. They believe in what they are doing and in what the job stands for. It may not turn out to be your niche or world, but respect them for what they love about theirs.
7   Being inquisitive and curious.
8   Accept feedback calmly.

You may not always like what you hear. Challenge the person giving feedback politely. *'This is a very tough industry and not many people make it to the starting blocks.'* Okay, so that may be the case, but clearly people *do* need to make it so you need to focus on that percentage – whatever it is – the 5, 10, 20 per cent of applicants – and find out just what it is that brings them success. Focus on the people who've succeeded, not on generalisations that *'It's difficult, it's tough'*. It may well be, but it's not impossible. Turn the negatives around to: *'It's difficult, but it's possible. It's tough but it's rewarding.'* Talk about the *'I can'* and *'I will'* rather than the *'I'll try'* or *'Maybe…'*. Ask people *'What is your perception of me?'* to get feedback on how you present yourself and how you come over. This will help give them something to remember you by. *'I met with a designer who was absolutely passionate about … really great ideas and done some terrific projects. You should give them a call – might be able to help you …'*.

What would be the cost to you if didn't achieve your career goals? Envisaging such an outcome can provide a terrific leverage to get you out of your comfort zone and make those phone calls and send the emails to make contacts. It can propel you into making that extra effort, going the extra mile and turning the last corner to find the right opening. What are you prepared to do in order to make sure it happens? How outlandish are you prepared to be in the way you tackle a situation, and how far out of your comfort zone are you prepared to go to make it happen? Your passion for your career and what you want to achieve should inspire and excite you so much that you're prepared to do what it takes to sell yourself. True networking is only really effective when you push yourself out of your comfort zone and think out of the box.

A key benefit to your networking activities will be to create and build a strong support team around you. Each person on your team should bring you something different. There will be members of your support team you've known all your life, such as your family, family friends and your friends. Within that group, there will be one or two people whom you trust perhaps just that little bit more than the rest. You know they will be open and honest with you and you also know you handle any constructive criticism from them because it's fair and just. Then there are people who fill you with energy, a 'can do' approach, who could inspire you to great things. Perhaps these may include your peers at university; how often have you sat about and brainstormed an idea late into the night which is going to make you all lots of money and bring you fame? Keep in regular contact with those friends who enable you to unlock your potential and your creativity. There will also be the people you (secretly) admire and consider your success and role models. They may be a member of your family, perhaps your mother or father; or they could be a high profile leader in business, politics, the community or someone with a 'go ahead' approach which fills you with energy and passion for your own beliefs and causes. Bring these people on board by studying their methods to achieve success. What did they sacrifice along the way to get to where they wanted to be? How did they focus? Why not contact them to ask them how they did it and what advice they have for you? Would they even act as a mentor to you? Finally, there are those who are not yet known to you – those people working in the sort of profession you want to be in, those who can advise you and help you along the way. It is here that the skill of networking truly comes into its own.

The benefits of networking

Networking is all about asking others to help you access information which will help you – or others – get to where you need to be. You can access information and decision makers. You can tap into those in the know who are most likely to know the answer you need – it's a bit like the 'phone a friend' lifeline on the UK television programme *Who Wants to be a Millionaire?* The contestants choose the friend who is mostly likely to know the answer to the question they are faced with, and it's the same here. You need to reach those beyond those you know and extend a line and call for information and help to those you *don't*.

This is the same in life. We all need the right people to call on in moments of crisis because we know they will give us the right support at that moment. We choose our friends because they have qualities we admire and enjoy. We elect to take some family members into our confidence as opposed to others because we know they have something slightly different to offer us, perhaps due to their life experience or their approach or attitude. As we go through life, we'll call on people at different times and there will be periods when we aren't in touch at all. Nonetheless, keep those fires of warmth and support burning because we know that when the time comes, we'll need to know we can pick up the telephone and call them or drop them an email to ask for help, even if it's just a friendly ear. Just the same way, there are people who know they can call on us.

Let's consider how networking can help you in your career. If you brainstorm all the people you know, whom you've met or watched at presentations as they came into your university, you can probably draw up a long list list, as shown in Figure 4.1.

Fifteen ways networking can help you in your career

1   Acquiring relevant work experience, especially in highly competitive sectors where contacts are everything.
2   Help with your CV, application or portfolio.
3   Information about a career or organisation, or better still, an introduction to someone working in it.
4   An idea of the skills, qualities and experience an employer wants and the personalities they recruit; would you be a good 'fit'?
5   How a sector works, e.g. the culture, behaviour, dress, language, values.
6   The name of the best recruitment agency for you to talk to.
7   Advice on the best way 'in' to a sector or company.
8   Projects an employer needs doing but does not have the resource internally to undertake which you could then volunteer for.
9   Tip-offs when a job comes up – many companies advertise their vacancies to staff first on their notice boards or company intranet.
10 Finding out what roles are available for new graduates.
11 Discovering the best place to look for vacancies.

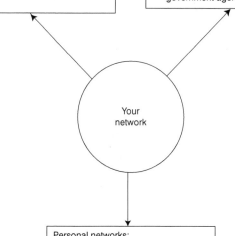

In the sector you want to work in:

- within a company
- across different companies in the sector
- universities to find out what's new and hot on the knowledge front
- university to university, if you're an academic
- professional bodies
- organisations devoted to the sector e.g. the IET
- cluster groups, on a national, regional and local basis
- graduate initiatives, e.g. Knowledge Transfer Partnership
- links between universities and employers

Networks dedicated to start-up businesses or helping graduates:

- the self-employed and small business networks such as the Federation of Small Businesses
- government bodies, e.g. BusinessLink
- cross-cultural networks and organisations
- organisations targeted at particular groups, e.g. Women In Rural Enterprises
- sector specific networks
- government agencies

Your
network

Personal networks:

- leisure and hobby interests
- voluntary and public sectors
- community service organisations, e.g. Soroptimists (women) and Rotary International
- friends and family
- professionals, e.g. doctors, dentists
- product and service providers you use, e.g. banks, builders, garages, etc.
- school, college, university
- religious organisations
- fellow students – could you do something together?

Figure 4.1

1   Discussing the industry overall, its strengths, weaknesses, opportunities and threats; the pros and cons of working in it and how it is structured.
2   Advice from small business owners as they reflect back on their own experiences of setting up. Did they make any mistakes they would warn others about?
3   Acquiring names of bodies and groups who are really helpful when setting up a business.
4   Learning the names of grants or funding you can tap into.

Many people don't push their network into unknown areas so never really truly reap the benefits networking can bring.

The danger of networking with fellow graduates is that if you're both in the same boat, you may simply spend time and energy bemoaning the current state you're in, which won't change anything. So if you're talking to a fellow graduate, have a good moan for five minutes and then spend 15 minutes brainstorming in which you can both change the situation you're in for the better and bounce ideas and contacts off each other. One of those ideas could be the breakthrough you've been looking for (see Figure 4.2).

Get pushy and ask for help – most people will be delighted to help you

Six steps to pro-active networking

1   Identify what you need to know or what sort of people you want to meet and why they are important to you.
2   Identify the people you *do know* and imagine on paper what their network would be like.
3   Make contact and ask for advice and help. If someone has referred you to a contact, mention their name.
4   Approach people you don't know but can find more easily through relevant professional organisations and trade associations.
5   Think big and laterally and you could connect to thousands of people worldwide at a stroke. The key is to secure introductions to the people in the right place.
6   Be open to asking for advice and help

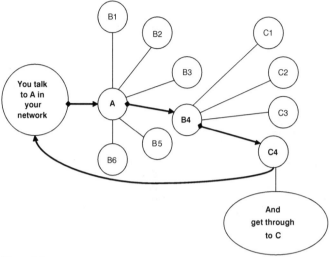

Figure 4.2

Professional organisations

Professional bodies exist partly to help promote the public's confidence in the professions they represent. As such, membership of a professional body may be essential to practice. They also help members and new entrants into the field to have satisfying and fulfilling careers, access to the right training and networks, and meet the challenges and opportunities that come their way. Many such organisations in the creative industries are listed under Useful Addresses at the end of this book.

Broadly speaking, professional bodies' sites may cover topics as shown in Table 4.1.

Most professional organisations are sympathetic to the job seeker, especially those from college or university, or returning to work. On initial contact, you may talk to a person employed by the professional body to be at the end of the phone, offering information and advice. They will have particular hints and advice for you, the new entrant, the career changer, the mature student and the young professional. They can also help point you in the direction of areas of their website which may be of interest and to local groups in your area. You can find many links from sites such as www.prospects. ac.uk.

Within a professional body's site, you will find links to further organisations which may be of interest to the visitor. Figure 4.3 gives examples.

Table 4.1

• Information about the organisation, its missions and goals	• Career case studies/role models
• A register of practitioners and their areas of expertise and specialism, often with their contact details	• Technical articles
	• Learning and education
	• Useful links
	• Information about the profession as a whole
• Events	• Library services
• Jobs search	• Annual conferences in the UK and abroad
• Online forum groups	
• Latest industry news	• Salary calculator
• Latest publications relevant to the industry	• Services available to the public
	• Vacancy listings
• Research	• Advice line on pricing issues
• Information for the public on the body, its standards, ethics and training	• Setting up on your own

Within each professional body, there will probably be a plethora of people with a particular niche interest. For example, this can get to be very specific indeed; within transport, for example, you may find aerospace, automotive and road transport systems, radar sonar and navigation and railways. There is nothing stopping you approaching a professional body to see if you can create your own forum or networking group.

You can access engineering/built environment forums from the sites of many professional and academic bodies and create lots of useful contacts through them, while learning from questions others raise. SCENTA (www.scenta.co.uk/careers) links through to a huge number of bodies and networks in industry and academia, educational exchanges, research, accreditation and evaluation and more. Sites and networking groups related to engineering and the built environment are listed at the back of this book. A site with a fantastic range of links, both UK and international, is that of the Commission for Architecture and the Built Environment (www.cabe.org.uk).

Join your alumni

Do it now; you'll find details on your university's website. Try tracking down past alumni who are working in sectors you want to join. They can answer many of your questions, give you advice and may be able to point you in the right direction for more help and support. Find out what they like and dislike about what they're doing,

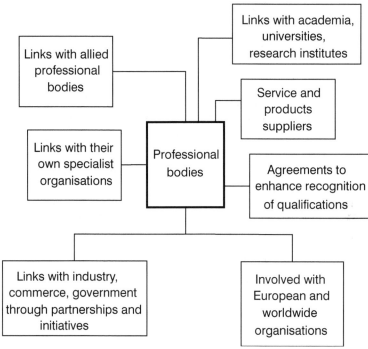

Figure 4.3

and what they see the challenges are from the point of view of their career and life. What appealed to them about the organisation they joined and how has the partnership fared so far? Where do they see it going in the future? Why not set up an e-group (you can do this through *Yahoo*, for example) of your fellow graduates to act as a focal point of ideas, contacts, support, advice and help?

Academic groups

Academics network across the world as much as professionals in the business field. Some of them were listed in the previous chapter, and more can be found under Useful Addresses at the back of this book. Academics attend conferences, listen to papers, give presentations, undertake joint research projects, compare notes, research, debate, argue, discuss, discover and invent. They talk on the phone, they email and they have their own networks across their universities, research institutes and other relevant organisations. They live and breathe their subjects, and they're encouraged to work with business, whether they like it or not, and to create a far more entrepreneurial spirit in their departments and students. You can tap into their networks by visiting universities' and research institutes' sites and looking for relevant links or talking to academics in the field to tap into their knowledge, or by checking with professional bodies. Examples are the Conference of European Schools for Advanced Engineering Education and Research (www.cesaer.org/) and the International Network for Engineering Education and Research (iNEER at www.ineer.org). There are also discipline networks, such as the European Civil Engineering Education and Training (EUCEET at www.euceet.utcb.ro).

You may be thinking that academic life is for you. Sites such as www.jobs.ac.uk have details of jobs in the higher education sector, as do institutions on their own websites. Your university may have affiliated networking groups which attend functions at it, or contribute to course development in one way or another, so make it your aim to find out what sort of organisations are connected with the university you've been studying at to see if there is a way you can link in with them.

Your department may have details of employers who routinely recruit students from your course; many do so year-on-year, because they know what you'll have been taught and the skills you'll have picked up, and they may even offer considerable input into your course development itself. This ensures the curriculum meets employers' needs.

Allied groups

There are a number of professional affiliates which participate in the development of the engineering profession offering opportunities to network with other bodies and access information on major issues affecting engineering and its profession. Examples include:

- Association for Project Management (www.apm.org.uk);
- Association of Cost Engineers (www.acoste.org.uk);
- Institute of Quality Assurance (www.iqa.org);
- Society of Automotive Engineers (www.sae-uk.org);
- Institute of Automotive Engineer Assessors (www.guideto. iaea.org.uk);
- Institute of Concrete Technology (ww.ictech.org).

The international picture

Many professional bodies are allied to international groups, thereby giving them a global view, network and contacts. Examples include:

* National Society of Professional Engineers (USA);
* Engineering Council (UK);
* ACSE (China);
* Engineering Australia;
* FEANI, ESOEPE and EurEta (Europe).

The benefits of joining an international body are many. You can acquire a new network of working colleagues and friends as you meet over emails but face-to-face too in meetings, conferences and working groups to thrash out ways forward. You can access information networks such as the EDN newsletter, Asian Report and cross-cultural networks and organisations such as FEANI in Europe. People often think they don't need an international network – until an occasion arises when they wish they did! Having colleagues and friends in your line of work (and outside it) can give you a very different outlook on the world and the opportunities within it. Reach out and offer a helping hand – you never know when your efforts will be repaid!

Women's groups

The Association for Women in Science, Engineering and Construction is just one example of a national organisation designed to promote careers in the sector for girls and women, to represent women's voices and provide a network for mutual support. An organisation such as this will also seek to act as a centre of information and resource and a forum for discussion and debate, with community support, a branch network, a forum magazine and news, views and links. Tap into networks such as this for any help and support on offer – if you can focus on the sort of help you're looking for, so much the better for you and for those who are able to help you. Learn from those who are where you want to be. Organisations such as AWISE also run conferences and may organise taster courses for those considering taking up a career in the sector and refresher courses for those seeking to return after a career break. They frequently network abroad, for example AWISE has connections in Australia, New Zealand, South Africa, France and Germany. For more information, see Useful Addresses at the end of this book. Groups such as these can be helpful throughout your career, and many provide refresher courses or help for those who have taken time out to have children and are now looking to return to work.

Women in Business networks forming gradually in the UK also offer the opportunity to meet with fellow businesswomen and talk business, network, hear speakers and exchange contact details.

Informal networks

As important as their formal peers, informal networks are the places to go to meet like-minded people who will cheer you up when you feel low, give you good, sound advice over a pint and talk about *the* latest design from the sector which is truly giving everyone the 'Wow!' factor. You may find these in coffee houses, bars, restaurants, pubs – any place where people in the sector hang out. You can also tap into informal networks through any social situation; remember that talking to an accountant over a drink, he may have clients in the sector who just could provide that right introduction for you.

What about websites?

You can access careers advice and information online and in person through a number of sites and these are listed under Useful Addresses through university careers services and government providers, plus sites such as www.prospects.ac.uk and www.hobsons.com. Wherever you are, visit or contact your local university's careers service and find out what help is available to you as a new graduate. Be specific about the help you need. Know the questions you want answers to. Go into careers interviews knowing what you want to cover. Be honest with yourself and others – this is not a test. In addition, there may be sites geared towards graduates in your particular region, such as GradSouthWest (www.gradsouthwest.com) in the south west of the UK (see Useful Addresses at the back of this book).

Websites such as www.futureskillsscotland.org.uk and www.futureskillswales.com can help signpost you in the direction of other sites, such as enterprise and business link agencies, to find out:

- local labour market information;
- national projections of skills in demand and how sectors will grow or not;
- initiatives to bring graduates and employers together which may or may not be independent of any national schemes;
- training on offer in your area;
- advice for those starting out;
- details of trade shows, training, events, help-lines, agencies and links;
- local networks, not necessarily allied to professional bodies and groups.

Look ahead, get involved

As technological advances take place at an ever increasing rate, so the opportunities for networking across borders and specialist areas multiply. They will take place to advance technology in its widest form and to stimulate innovation and growth. They may be government driven, or research and university led; or come about through the merger and acquisition of various companies.

One site which would enable you to truly get involved and make a difference is that of the International Young Professionals Foundation (www.iypf.org/). Make a difference to the world and network with people like yourself worldwide in all sorts of sectors and roles. Based in Australia, it works in the field of human rights, poverty eradication and environment and social capitalisation in the broader context of sustainability. The Commonwealth has lots of other opportunities (www.cec.org).

Start-ups

There are also websites for the small business and start-ups, such as the Federation of Small Businesses (www.fsb.org.uk), the Small Business Service (www.sbs.gov.uk), Start-Ups (www.startups.co.uk) and BusinessLink (www.businesslink.gov.uk). They can all signpost you in the right direction and they are listed at the back of this book. These will enable you to make friends and potential clients, customers or employers over the Internet.

Make the most of professional bodies

Professional bodies' discussion forums are very useful to see what the hot topics are and to be able to comment on them at interviews or assessment days. It is not uncommon for people to ask for careers advice through these forums. Many organisations have local networks with regular meetings (sometimes with a speaker), events, training programmes and newsletters. There may also be visits to businesses for a look around, or a social gathering. Most will enable members to talk to each other and catch up, meet new people or give each other referrals.

Go on – attend a meeting in your area

It is in the organisation's interests to show you goodwill and interest and yours to represent yourself in a professional manner. Dress in business attire – suit and tie – and practice good social skills – a warm, firm handshake, a smile and lots of eye contact. Ask questions – what people do, who do they work for, what sort of clients do they have. If they give you their business card, follow it up with an email saying something like 'It was nice to meet you – would it be possible for us to meet up? – I'd love to talk you further about ...'. Be ready to talk positively about your course, the projects you did and that you are currently working on, and your career plans, and people who inspire you. Mention articles you've seen in the press or online which show you're up-to-date and show enthusiasm and interest. Find out before you go about any initiatives in your area which are running to strengthen the relationship between graduates and small employers – it could just help swing the mind of a small employer to give a graduate like you a chance, if only if he or she had some guidance on how to make the most of you.

If the thought of attending such a meeting fills you with horror...

Why not contact the person in charge of your local group to explain that you're coming along for the first time and to ask for someone to look out for when you arrive to introduce yourself to? There should be someone there whose role it is to welcome new members and make them feel at home. Look out for them, and ask them to introduce you to someone who is working in a specific area that you'd like to get involved with. Find out in advance who will be there, and head for those you most want to talk to when you arrive, armed with prepared questions. Be interested and you'll soon forget your own nerves. Remember that you're with a group of like-minded people who may well remember what it's like to start out. They're on your side. Ask to meet them to find out more. Identify specific questions to ask before you go so that it is clear you have given the meeting some thought and prepared well for it. Be chatty and interested, passionate and enthusiastic, keen and self-motivated and you'll attract help and support, but remember you may need to go out of your way to find it.

Successful networking

Open-mindedness and generosity is crucial, but be discerning too. Listen to what people have to say, and then assess the information and feedback you're getting against what's important to *you* and your criteria.

Ten more steps to successful networking

1 Don't assume the information you're getting is current. Don't assume those you're talking to are up-to-date. Go that extra mile by checking with professional bodies and trade associations.

2 Guard your safety. If you're meeting someone, do so in a public place or in their office premises. Visit the company's website to make sure their address is valid. Don't give too many personal details out over the Internet or telephone.

3 Present yourself to the highest standard possible using business behaviour and language. Dress in your interview suit then examine your image from head to toe in front of a long mirror at home. If you're self-employed, think about the image you want to portray about your business.

4 Use networking to digest strategies which will put you ahead of the competition, whether you're looking for a new job or starting and developing your own business.

5 Networking is a two-way process. When people help you, see if there is anything you can do to help them. Build on the relationships you develop. Treat others as you would like to be treated yourself.

6   If you are at a networking event, spend about five minutes talking to the person you're with and then move on. You are *all* there to meet as many people as possible, so close the conversation. *'It's been nice to meet you. Shall we exchange cards and move on?'*

7   What perception do you want the people you meet to have of you? Do you want to come over as someone who takes their career and chosen field seriously and passionately, or as someone who's out to have a good time? Are you portraying yourself to be someone who can be trusted and loyal?

8   Don't give the impression that you hop from one company to another too often. It costs employers money to recruit staff and they won't be too impressed if you arrive, work for a year or so, and then move on. Word gets around about job-hoppers. Be discreet if you're looking elsewhere for opportunities.

9   Set yourself goals for each networking opportunity. What do you want to achieve from it? Divide your networks in groups and give each group a goal for the week or month. Measure your success. What are you doing that is yielding the best results?

10   Keep in touch with people in your network. Email them from time to time to ask how they are and how things are going. A network is only as active and alive as you make it.

Go out there and immerse yourself in the fabric and make-up of those working in the sector you want to get into.

Whatever you choose to do, be it related to your degree or otherwise, aim to build up a very strong understanding of the world you want to work in and seek to identify who really knows the local scene and has an influence in it. Informal networks are as important as those which are of a professional foundation, so find out where people meet in your sector online and face-to-face and get involved. It's a great chance to meet with like-minded people who share the same passions you do and they will cheer you up when you're feeling low and point you in the direction of all sorts of useful resources.

Networking is for life!

Use your networks to build key relationships in the sectors in which you want to work. Nurture them. Networking skills make a difference to your career and life, particularly in industries where the percentage of people working on projects or contracts is high. If you're running a small business, you need a strong network of people who will lead you to suppliers, potential customers and clients. As an academic, you'll network with others involved in your subject.

Networking is as important outside a company as you move up the career ladder as it is in it. Many senior managers and professionals are recruited through recruitment agencies, head-hunters and search companies. These companies receive assignments from organisations who have roles to fill. Head-hunters will call around their contacts in the industry to see if they know of anyone who might fit the bill. Someone in your network may think of you.

Network for your life, not just your career

As well as networking within your sector, you'll have a fine balance in life if you develop networks of friends and colleagues outside it. This is important if you wish to gain new clients as a sole trader or the senior partner or managing director of a company. Most people would rather select someone they know to do a job than a total unknown. Industry and personal contacts matter. Either way, you need to decide how to promote your services. In this instance, you could consider attending local events put on to help business people network and exchange business cards so that they can pick up on each other's services and how they may help businesses. Local networking events targeting small businesses may help. Explore the networks in your area and on the Internet, and assess which ones will be most appropriate to you. They may also provide continuing professional development which could count towards your annual development hours essential to maintain your professional status.

Networking can be very helpful in all sorts of ways including:

1 finding specialist expert health advice;
2 locating the estate agent who will really get your house sold fast and is always the first to hear of houses coming onto the market;
3 getting your children into the right school;
4 looking after ageing relatives and making the system work to your advantage;
5 volunteering to give something back;
6 meeting people of like mind, such as knowing where the places are to go to meet fellow artists and designers;

7   asking about hotels for that special holiday next year;
8   meeting new people at the pub, in the gym and through your
    interests;
9   learning something new and keeping your life fresh and ac-
    tive;
10 having fun and giving something back at the same time.

Summary action points

The way you network at every level can affect the flavour and fabric
in your life so make it a priority.

1   What network groups are there in your area which you can
    make contact with and get involved with? List them and make
    that first contact.
2   Find out if they have mentors to help people like yourself who
    want to get into the sector. If they do, ask if you can be al-
    located one.
3   Contact five people in your network. Ask if they know of any-
    one who could help you. Arrange to meet for a coffee to catch
    up with them or organise an information meeting.

Chapter 5

Hunting out the right opportunity

So far, you've ascertained what you want to do – now you need to work out how and where you want to do it.

How important is the 'where?' to you?

What factors are driving your decision in terms of where you live? Many UK graduates move abroad to find the lifestyles and career opportunities they want – and what have they got to lose? The choices shown in Table 5.1 can all impact on your future life and the opportunities within it, so consider which option in each line is most important to you. This is also a good test of how important your career is to you compared with the other elements in life. Would you move tomorrow to where the right career opportunities were for you, regardless of where that was?

Other factors which will impact on your lifestyle are your access to cultural activities, sports and leisure interests, the make up of local people and quality of life in the area. You are unlikely to find somewhere which meets all of these criteria so some degree of compromise will be required. If your career matters to you above all else, you'll move to where the sector is strong and growing fast as opposed to where it is non-existent.

Whether you plan to be self-employed or work for someone else, be alert to opportunity

Watch the world carefully and keep up-to-date with events and trends. Are there any booming economies which would benefit from your skills and talents? Events which can be disastrous for some people provide huge opportunities for others. For example,

Table 5.1

Near friends	Same town as friends	Ready to make new friends and keep in touch with old ones
Close to family	Living with parents	Irrelevant – we email and text and they can visit
Cost of living low	Cost of living irrelevant – salary will match	Need to keep this in mind – must find out what living costs are
Opportunity to live cheaply to pay back loans	Have bills, but then doesn't everyone?	Not as important as the job itself
Sector I want to go into is strong in the region with lots of employers	I'll take my chances – I want to stay in the city I did my degree in. I'll take what I find	I'm ready to go to the other side of the world to get the job I want
Staying in home country	Want to go abroad	If the job takes me abroad, so be it
City	Town	Countryside/rural
Irrelevant – the job comes first	Have a strong preference for where I live	Am absolutely living in this city regardless of opportunities
Short commute to work	Commute is irrelevant – it's the job and employer which matters	Willing to commute within reason

a company makes 500 people redundant, that's unfortunate for the 500 but a great business opportunity for careers coaches and redundancy advisers. Similarly, the Olympics in Beijing in 2008 and in London in 2012 will offer great opportunities for people with the right skills. Some 33,000 additional jobs will be created in London thanks to the Olympics, and civil engineers and specialist skills will be in particular demand.

You can pick up more news, developments and information from sites such as:

- Biomedical Engineering Online (www.biomedical-engineering-online.com/);
- Building Services and Environmental Engineer (www.bsee.co.uk);

- www.e4engineering.com (engineering, design and industry news 24 hours a day);
- Electronics Weekly (www.electronicsweekly.co.uk);
- Engineering News Record – worldwide construction news (www.enr.com);
- New Civil Engineer magazine, daily updates (www.nceplus.co.uk);
- Mechanical Engineering Magazine (www.memagazine.org/);
- Nuclear Engineering Magazine (www.neimagazine.com/);
- The Chemical Engineer magazine (www.tcetoday.com);
- Technology and computing news online (www.zdnet.com)

Also the following journals:

- *New Civil Engineer* (weekly, EMAP);
- *The Structural Engineer, Institution of Structural Engineers* (fortnightly).

For a list of journals:

- *American Society of Mechanical Engineers* (http://www.asme.org/Publications/Journals/View_Journals_Online.cfm).

What's the picture in the UK?

Like every other sector, the engineering and built environment sectors have their hot spots in the UK. Current labour market intelligence which you can access through government websites can be very helpful. The good news is that there will be a significant increase in demand for those at the higher skilled end of the work force, such as managers, professionals, associate professionals and those engaged in technical and service occupations.

Every sector has its hot spots and weak parts. You can find out where your sector's hot spots are by looking at government websites relating to trade and industry, the economy and sites such as the UK Trade and Investment (www.invest.uktradeinvest.gov.uk/) but also in each of the Regional Development Agencies' (RDAs') websites. The RDAs in England have been created to ensure strong and sustainable economic growth and success, while ensuring quality of life and opportunity for those living in the area. They have their equivalents in Scotland, Wales and Northern Ireland. There are also European

RDAs (www.eurada.org). Look for labour market information at the regional and national level which will point you in the direction of the hot spots. In areas of traditional and declining industries, redundant skills and depleting resources, RDAs are responding by leading and creating initiatives in such areas by regenerating them, boosting learning opportunities and facilitating skill acquisition and start-ups. Cluster groups and localised graduate websites (see Further Information at the end of this book) may direct you to useful local networks. Sites such as www.semta.org.uk has lots of information about sector strategy groups, plus labour market assessments, training frameworks and occupational standards, as do other sector skills councils which you can access from www.ssda.org.uk.

What initiatives are available to encourage employers to take on graduates?

Governments are investing a lot of money in developing skills and talent, and particularly so at the graduate end of the market in areas where business and commerce can really benefit from the transfer of knowledge and fresh input. There are many initiatives, programmes, events, websites, help-lines, networking groups, advisory services and more to help you and your peers. In the UK, for example, RDAs are encouraging universities and businesses alike to retain skilled talent in their area and working to raise small companies' awareness of how graduates can benefit them. There is a strong connection between the skill levels in an area and the quality of working opportunities and lifestyle on offer which is why huge efforts are being made to regenerate those areas which are lagging behind. These bodies are also trying to encourage inward investment which should create more employment opportunities. Consider initiatives such as the Knowledge Transfer Partnerships (www.ktponline.org.uk/graduates) which enable graduates and post-graduates to undertake a project within a company while acquiring management training or working towards further industry specific qualifications or even post-graduate studies. The initiative aims to promote enterprise, creativity and innovation. Graduates work on a project such as re-assessing how products are made, operating procedures and product development. The difference they are making to organisations and companies is dramatic. Ask about Graduate Apprenticeship schemes which enable you to make the link between university and the workplace, building up your transferable skills, professional competence, technical expertise and management potential.

Many regional graduate careers service providers (see Useful Addresses at the end of this book) offer work placement programmes and schemes designed to boost your employability. This forms part of their drive to encourage graduates to remain in the area after their degree studies. Tap into them because they will help smooth your path through offering workshops, initiatives, practical advice and information which could be the difference between you struggling on and getting there eventually or taking the fast path to success.

What support is available from local business or government groups?

Watch out for initiatives and support available. The names of these may change; some may be driven under the direction of one body one year (such as the Design Council in the UK) and then transferred over to another, perhaps a university, in the following year. Some may be targeted to areas in which strenuous efforts are being made to regenerate the economy.

Search out suitable employment opportunities

How much do you know about the companies in the sectors you are applying to?

- ◆ Where do they tend to be based? Does one region of the country or world tend to have a monopoly?
- ◆ Who are the companies in that sector? What size are they? What do they do? Who are their clients? What is happening in the area to encourage companies like them to take graduates?
- ◆ How do they recruit? Large corporates will probably have a graduate recruitment department with deadlines and lots of hoops to jump through, including assessment centres. A small company is likely to have the boss, to whom you can send your CV and a covering letter in print or by email. Are there agencies in the region which are relevant to the sector and, if so, who are they? What is their track record and how long have they been practising in the sector?

Employers use a range of methods to recruit employees and you should use a range of methods in your job hunting. Consider how employers recruit. They could enlist freelances or temps to save them taking on staff long term. But they also have a range of other options open to them, including linking with schools, colleges and universities through careers fairs and presentations, their own websites or those of agencies, advertisements in the local press, looking at on-spec applications, finding students through work experience, internships and secondments. They could spread the net wider, hooking potential recruits in through agencies, the national press, specialist trade journals; some are even using Radio and TV adverts.

Hint: You can do a search for businesses at http://local.google. com/. Use several search terms to maximise the effectiveness of your search.

If you use a multitude of methods to find employers and seek the role you crave, you're more likely to land it. Stick to one or two, and you're going to have a harder trek. Walk into every circle shown in Figure 5.1 to hunt for the opportunities you're looking for and persist in your efforts until you find success.

In addition, you should:

1   run a search for all the relevant employers using all the means at your disposal, including Kompass and Dun and Bradstreet, both have excellent online resources of businesses and company information;

2   check out graduate listings such as Prospects Directory, Prospects Today, Prospects Finalist, The Hobsons Directory; Technology Horizons (www.technologyhorizons.com) and careers service vacancy listings;

3   use your local library which should have sector reports, books and information about the local area, trade and national magazines and phone and trade directories, including *Consultant Engineers* and *Technologists 500* and *The Structural Engineer*;

4   register for any email alerts with online agencies to pick up new jobs which come in that might interest you.

Many online sites have job searches and vacancy listings. The online magazine Project Manager is one of these (www.PMstaff. co.uk). Another site to visit is that of Construction Plus, which is the

Take action:
Plan; search; identify; contact; join; find out; ask; enthuse; listen; create

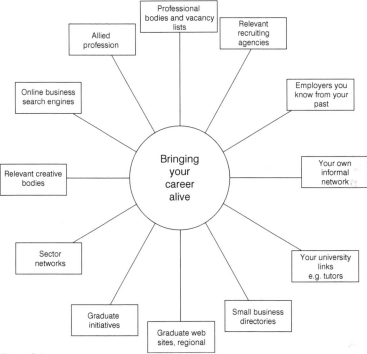

Figure 5.1

Internet arm of the Emap construction network. It brings together the various assets of Emap's magazines, including *The Architects' Journal, Construction News, New Civil Engineering* and *QS Week*. It has invaluable databases including news stories, web and magazine articles and construction vacancies and a database of over 30,000 construction companies and organisations. There's also RUDI (Resource for Urban Design Information) and www.urbandesignjobs. com which has coverage of both the private and public sector nationally and internationally with a specialism in or knowledge of urban design. The website www.thecareerengineer.com has vacancies and recruitment information and www.project-management-jobs. com/ has vacancy listings and help with CV writing and selling yourself. The website www.careersinconstruction.com has a graduate section which invites employers to search for raw and experienced graduates and graduates-to-be and for graduates to search out job opportunities. Many more sites are listed under Useful Addresses at the end of this book.

'I want to work abroad!'

Working abroad requires considerable research and preparation if you're to have the experience you want. Recruitment companies who have an international reach often have advice on their sites about moving abroad. The website www.asia.hobsons.com has information on working in China, Taiwan, Thailand, Hong Kong, Singapore, Malaysia, Indonesia and Japan with market trends and industry summaries, and overall regional outlooks plus details of events in the area. Prospects (www.prospects.ac.uk) has numerous country profiles, incorporating details on the job market, international companies in the region you're reading about, language requirements, work experience, vacancy sources and visa and immigration information. See Further Reading at the end of this book for useful suggestions.

Questions to ask yourself

1   What do you want to get out of the experience? What is your reason for going?

2   Where do you want to work? Do you want to take the opportunity to learn a new language or improve existing language skills?

3   What do you want to do? Do you want to work for an employer in a job which will contribute to your career progression or simply go apple picking for six months?

4   How different do you want the culture of the country you're going to be working to be from your own?

5   How will your current qualifications be regarded in the country you plan to work in – will you need to get any additional 'top up' qualifications to meet their own regulations and criteria to work as a practising professional?

6   What visa requirements will there be? What happens about health insurance? What are the tax implications for you while working abroad and when you return home?

7   Can you do it under the auspices of your current or a future employer?

8   How long do you want to do it for?

Go on the alert for vacancies

Of course you can register your details with various online agencies, associations and groups, which have the facility to enable employers to search out someone with the skills and talents they need. This does work, and also gives you the opportunity to receive email alerts when new jobs come in and to browse the vacancies available and make contact with the appropriate agency or employer.

Going through recruitment companies

Recruitment agencies are selected by employers to find recruits for them. Many employers have long-standing relationships with agencies, so agency consultants build up an extensive knowledge of what the employer is like to work for and what sort of career path candidates can expect upon successful application and starting.

Agencies offer various services to their candidates, including help with CVs (although some agencies have their own particular CV format to send to clients) and profiling so that you can work out what sort of work would suit you best. Your consultant should have a clear idea of trends in the sector, and how your career will fit into it, and he or she should enjoy strong links with the industry. Many offer training, and some run networking evenings. It's essential to remember that your consultant is human, too, so treat him or her as you would like to be treated.

Online recruitment has become big business. Many online agencies and professional bodies offer the facility of sending email alerts, enabling you to receive notice that new (relevant) vacancies are available. Newspapers and trade magazines also have online vacancy boards and often send newsletters. You may also be able to post your CV on some sites for potential employers to view.

If you want to get into a specific industry, look for agencies which are active in and focus on it, with a good track record – they are more likely to have a strong network and an ear to the ground for opportunities. The Recruitment and Employment Confederation has lists of agencies handling specific sectors; you could also visit www.constructionplus.co.uk and Thomas Telford (www.t-telford. co.uk). You can quickly access a huge number of agencies in specific sectors by visiting www.agencycentral.co.uk which has both agencies listed under sector and also has a full list of agencies offering graduate positions.

If you have any complaints concerning the way your agency handles you, your CV or the process, take it up with the agency itself. You can also, however, contact bodies such as the Recruitment and Employment Confederation (REC), the professional body for the recruitment sector. Find out how your CV is circulated by the consultant: is it sent out ad hoc in the hope it will interest employers, or to those who are actually recruiting? Is it sent without your prior knowledge or does the consultant discuss with you who to send it out to based on responding to specific, live vacancies? Or will he discuss what he plans to do with it with you before sending it out at all, live vacancies or not? There have been cases of consultants sending out CVs to an individual's employer, which clearly jeopardises the position of the individual in that company.

Go to where the action is, ready to sell your talents and knowledge

This includes careers events and trade fairs, not just those surrounding the area of employment, and shows anywhere you are likely to find companies involved in the business. These may be run by the DTI in the UK, the sector skills councils (www.ssda.org.uk), industry specific professional bodies, careers services or professional tradeshow organisers who have identified a need for an event. They all have their own slant and mission: some may be held to bring companies together to discuss and exchange ideas, products and services. There are also conferences which enable professionals and researchers to share and develop their expertise. They will provide a forum for you to get out there, meet and greet and hand people your business card.

You can find a list of the larger shows (details by industry, date and/or region) at:

- www.biztradeshows.com;
- www.eventseye.com;
- your local business network sites listing sector specific events and exhibitions
- www.exhibitions.co.uk (UK).

If you're planning to go as an exhibitor, www.businesslink.gov.uk has some first-class tips on how to make the most of a show.

Fairs and exhibitions may be specialist in nature (e.g. Engineering and IT specific) or they may be generic, covering a wide range of careers. These are not necessarily organised by university careers services – local services may also run fairs for the general public at which there will be far fewer graduates. The graduate fairs take place all over the country, often with a sector focus, such as the African Caribbean Diversity Fair; finance and management; Engineering Science and IT; Alternatives Fair; Volunteering fair; Law; and teaching and work experience. For more information, check out the following:

* the Prospects website at www.prospects.ac.uk;
* the Institute of Physics, Science, Engineering and Technology Careers Fair held annually (www.iop.org for more information);
* www.engineerjobs.co.uk; and
* www.semta.org.uk/semta.nsf/?Open will take you to details of the National Engineering Recruitment Exhibition.

There are many exhibitions where you can meet employers, so think laterally and go to where graduates might not normally go so that you can really stand out.

Plan for a successful event

When you approach stand-holders, an introductory chat about their company and what it's developing and working on can quickly lead to a sentence or two about yourself and your career goals. Regardless of whether you're going to a trade show or careers event, tips for a successful show include:

* Pre-register online to avoid lengthy queues.
* Identify the people you want to meet and visit their websites *before* you go. On arrival, visit their stands *first* while you're fresh and full of energy.
* Create a business card to hand out. Put your contact details (email and mobile number) and your most recent or relevant educational qualification on one side with niche areas; and the sort of company you're looking to work for plus skills you have to contribute on the other.

- Prepare questions to ask before you go to avoid mumbling and stumbling over awkward introductory waffle. *'What advice do you have for someone in my position?'* and *'What job hunting strategies can you suggest I use?'* can be two helpful questions to get insider information and give you other routes to follow.
- Ask open questions. *'Do you recruit graduates of any discipline?'* is a closed question requiring a simple yes or no answer; you won't learn much. *'What degrees do you particularly look to recruit?'* is hard to answer with a yes or no. As an open question, it gives you more information and enables you to engage the person you're talking to in further conversation.
- Don't start off by asking *'What can your company do for me?'* or *'What can your company offer me?'* Promote yourself as someone who has a lot to contribute to the right employer.
- If someone looks busy, wait until they are quieter.
- Talk to people in the café areas. Make some small talk about the fair – *'What a great opportunity to meet people!' 'What a great venue!' 'Isn't it good to sit down?' 'Are you here as an exhibitor?' 'What does your company do?' 'I'll stop by and see you at your stand!' 'Could I contact you next week and ask for some of your time?'* Smaller companies may not have a stand, but you might bump into a representative from one if you start talking to people in the café areas.
- If you get stuck talking to people who are being negative about your general situation, *'There are too many of us graduating!'* politely say goodbye and wish them luck and walk away. Focus on what you *do* want and ways to increase your chances of succeeding in getting it. Sitting and moping isn't going to make your dreams happen.
- When the event is over, walk away and reflect over what you've learnt about the opportunities available and yourself. Bring together action points and carry them through. Business cards create dust if unused; you want them to create results.
- Write and thank the people you met at the show by email or letter. If you have a web CV, you can attach the address under your contact details at the bottom. After the event, identify those people you need to follow up and contact them.

Your next steps

1 List employers in the sector you wish to work in to research and the country you want to work in.
2 Develop a short list by researching them. Continue your research through the Internet, careers fairs, finding out about their products and services, your network and news items.
3 Who do you know, or which sector networks could you tap into, to acquire an introduction to these companies?
4 Where might you meet people from them?
5 Have you got newsletters and/or vacancy alerts coming through to your inbox from:
   ◆ professional bodies
   ◆ relevant companies
   ◆ research institutes
   ◆ e-zines
   ◆ reports from the main sectors
   ◆ forums on sites of those bodies relevant to you
   ◆ printed press and trade magazines?

Moving things forward ... do you, don't you?

Find out more about the organisation and its career opportunities, but don't confine your research to the company's website. Delve further and wider for any mention of it in the local, national or international media. Most employers try to provide as much information as they can about their organisation to job hunters so that the latter can ensure they are applying to the right sort of company for them. Why not see if you can get in touch with someone appropriate at the company to see if you can visit and look around, and talk about the opportunities available?

Questions to ask of an employer

1 What is its mission and what does it want to do and achieve? Does it excite you?
2 What messages does it give you about its values and what it deems to be important? What values does the organisation or company portray in its advertising, literature, image and

brand? Look for evidence that it upholds these values. Do they excite you?

3   What is the size of the organisation and how will that impact on the way people work and the opportunities within it? What does it say about how to apply for work?

4   Where is it located? Is it spread over a number of sites?

5   What is the structure and hierarchy; is there just the one company or are there a number of subsidiary companies within one group?

6   How is it organised? A small company may have one person looking after IT, marketing, sales, web design and HR which would put a generalist business degree to excellent use; a large one will have a department of people for each of these elements enabling you to focus on one area.

7   What is the company's financial position? If it is not healthy, your career there may be short. What are its strengths, weaknesses, opportunities and threats?

8   What sort of people work for it? Look at employee profiles. What do they get involved with outside of work? How do they describe themselves, the company and their roles?

9   What is the company doing to be innovative and competitive? If there is no evidence of such activities, ask yourself whether it will exist in five years' time. How could you contribute to the company's overall business development and expansion? Careful research into its finances and diplomatic questioning at interview time can help you make an assessment.

10 What sorts of projects and products are they working on and how do these excite you?

Eight key questions to ask yourself

1   What could you contribute to this organisation in terms of skills and qualities?

2   What is it about the company that you would look forward to every Monday morning?

3   Could you see yourself working for them in five years' time?

4   What excites you about the direction it is heading in?

5   What would you need to do to make your career progress as you would like and what support would you get from the company?

6   What is the organisation's view on work–life balance and what specific examples are there to support this?

7   How could you secure a foot in the door?

8   Is there a vacancy right now you could apply for or will you need to make contact on spec?

If you're getting positive answers, a further question to ask yourself is: What actions are you going to take next and when?

If you're not going to take further action this time, you need to continue your search or adapt your views of the sort of role and company you're looking for.

Starting your own business

There is more help around than ever before for those with an entrepreneurial spirit but still too many start-ups fail for lack of sufficient advice and research. The BusinessLink network in England, helps small companies and start-ups. Visit www.businesslink.gov.uk to find your local link. There's information on setting up a business, writing a business plan, accessing funding, growing your business and even selling it on. There are also links to the sister organisations in Scotland, Wales and Northern Ireland.

Consider initiatives

Aside from Flying Start (see page 46), other national examples of organisations helping people to set up on their own include Shell LiveWIRE, the Prince's Trust, Start-ups and the Prime Initiative for the over 50s (see Useful Addresses at the end of this book). Some initiatives may be national in nature, others very local. As an example, the National Endowment for Science, Technology and the Arts (NESTA) announced a scheme to support graduates to build new types of companies and business markets. Visit www.nesta.org.uk/academy for more information.

Eight questions to consider

1   What's your vision and what do you want to achieve with this business?

2   What are your products and services?

3 What do you need to get up and running, e.g.:
   * somewhere to work from;
   * equipment needed to set up (you may have a lot of this already);
   * computer/lap top/ipod;
   * communications – Internet, phone, fax;
   * marketing and publicity materials, e,g. a website, business cards, brochures, membership of professional and business networks;
   * insurance, professional indemnity and public liability;
   * training;
   * a salary/wage?
4 Who can support you?
5 What new skills and knowledge will you need?
6 Who are your competitors?
7 What research do you need to do?
8 Where will you get funding from?

Summary action points

Move your thinking further forward:

1 What are agencies in the region doing to encourage businesses to take on graduates, particularly those in my sector?
2 How much do I know about the work I want to do and how to get 'in' to it?
3 Where are most of the employers located in this sector?
4 Which other areas are showing a rapid growth?
5 What am I doing to enjoy life and have time out while I'm working towards my goals?

Chapter 6

Proving yourself
From scholar to worker

One minute you're a student and the next you're not. You may choose to have some time out or get going on your career straightaway, but whichever path you take, there's a big difference between the two. The earlier you start preparing for life after your university days, the easier it will be to settle in work and life afterwards.

Making the psychological switch

There is quite a switch from being a student to becoming an employee, because the impact of your work and how well you do it affects other people, as shown in Table 6.1.

The 'learning to do' referred to above relates to those things you cannot be taught until you start work, such as product knowledge specific to the organisation you join. But at the very least, employers want to know that you know how to behave at work and that you understand what work is like.

At work, you'll still get the person who does it all the last minute, those who are indecisive, bullies, patronising or negative, who spout *'We've always done it like this'*, and see no reason to change. There are the moody, sulky and lazy, working alongside power-crazy, highly competitive workaholics and you'll need to deal with them all. Your skills and talents in motivating and managing people will be well tested as you progress and work to bring out the best in your team. You'll need your influencing and persuading skills to encourage those around you to see the benefits of what you want to do. But your experiences at university will have given you a good start in speaking up for yourself and getting along with people from all different backgrounds and with their own aspirations. Add work experience in a real live work situation, and you can put the above skills into place and make the psychological switch.

Table 6.1

As a student		As an employee
Studying	*and*	Working
Being a student	*and*	an employee/employer
Learning	*and*	Doing or learning to do ...
Student responsibilities	*and*	Responsibilities at work to-wards: team; clients, customers; company/employer; your own colleagues, peers
The hours you choose to work	*and*	The hours you're expected to work
Holidays	*and*	Average 4 weeks holiday – in the US, probably 1 or 2 weeks in the first few years
The way you dress and behave	*and*	The image and behaviour that's right and appropriate for work
Long-term personal goals	*and*	Vision, mission, targets need the goodwill and motivation of every-one on board
Rules and regulations in your university	*and*	Employment laws, health ands safety, professional regulations
Meeting deadlines – it's just you that suffers	*and*	Meeting deadlines – other people are depending on you
The pace of life – you can dictate it	*and*	The pace of work is dictated by the industry and demands of cli-ents and customers. Your day can change dramatically on receipt of a phone call. People expect fast responses. Are you adaptable and flexible?
Your performance – it affects just you	*and*	Your performance can affect that of your team and the company – it can clinch a deal, save the company money
You can control pretty much most things in your life	*and*	There are many things you can control but equally there are many you cannot

Transferable skills are essential to enjoy life and excel at work

List everything you've done during your university days and you will be astonished at what you've achieved formally and informally. To do it all, you'll have used skills which transfer from one aspect of life to another, such as communication. To communicate effectively with clients and colleagues, family and friends, you need to express yourself clearly, orally and in writing through email, letter and fax. You need to be able to empathise with and understand the needs of others. As an engineer or designer, for example, you will need to take a brief from a client, to redefine it and understand you have the scope of the matter to hand, and then come up with a solution for the client. You're solving their problem for them.

Rank the transferable skills in Figure 6.1 in order of your strength, 5 being the strongest.

Now find evidence for each one, looking through your list of extra-curricular activities, voluntary efforts, work experience and

	5	4	3	2	I
Organising/planning					
Communicating, orally					
Communicating, written					
Learning					
Creativity					
Decision making					
Self-motivation					
Strategic planning					
Handling change					
Problem solving					
Team working					
Leadership					
Adaptability, flexibility					
Self-awareness					
Commercial awareness					

Figure 6.1

academic work. Which are your strengths? Which are your weaknesses and how are you tackling those? Take each transferable skill and give an example of a time when you've used it. Consider all the angles you might be asked about it.

Have you made the most of university life?

University days offer the chance to create a life out of a blank canvas. Employers will be looking to see how you occupied your time and what you learnt from your activities. They'll be looking for evidence of your passion for your subject, such as any shows you've been to, any competitions you've entered and what projects you have done over and above your coursework. What were the modes of learning you used which could transfer over to the workplace, such as giving presentations, undertaking research, debating a point in seminars and tutorials, critiquing your work, taking an idea from conception to fruition, working in a team to solve a problem? How did you apply the theory you learnt in the classroom to real live working situations and problems or challenges in life.

Effectiveness and high performance at work is built on the right attitude, a professional competence and approach, product and sector knowledge, a *drive* to make things happen and soft skills. At university, you develop skills through various academic and extra-curricular activities. To progress your career, you need continued exposure to different experiences and the right training and personal development, all of which continue to expand your capabilities, push back your comfort zones and build on your soft or transferable skills. Self-awareness, self-promotion and self-presentation also count, along with keeping abreast of career developments and news in your field. Figure 6.2 shows how university and work link together incorporating all these elements, and don't forget that technical expertise also plays a part, depending on the sector you are in.

This extends beyond work!

Throughout your life, both in and out of work, you'll need to manage a number of ingredients, as shown in Table 6.2.

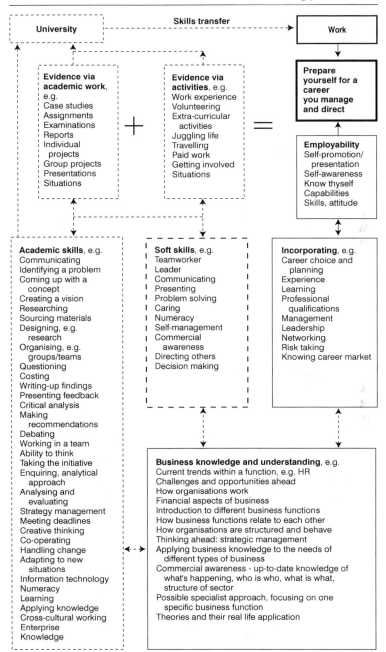

Figure 6.2

Table 6.2

Yourself	Information technology
People	Resources
Teams	Materials
Time	Projects
Money	Deadlines
Your energy	Research
The client's expectations	The facilities around you
Your future	Your suppliers

Who are you?

This is not just about your qualifications and experience to date. They certainly contribute and play a part, but this is more about how you arrived at the whole-rounded individual you are now. It's not about *'Well, I completed my UCAS form and made my six choices, and then sat and prayed that I'd get in to my first choice!'* It's about, how did you come to apply at all? What and who moulded your decisions and what did you need *within yourself* to get to where you are today? What resources did you pull out of your body, heart, mind and soul to make your degree happen and how can you build on them and use them to maximum effect throughout your life? Who did you work alongside as you strove to achieve your mutual goals? *(That's teamwork!)*

It's also about your values, and what matters to you. After all, you must have chosen the path you took for a reason. So what lies behind and within you, what makes you tick, what drives, inspires and motivates you. What challenges and dramas have you faced? How have you tackled them? *(That's problem solving.)* If you wrote your life story, what particular achievements would you want your readers to know about? What journeys would you want to tell them about? How can you show them that you've turned your plans into action? Have you done a stint of travelling, or juggled study and work at the same time? *(Shows adaptability and flexibility, planning and organisation.)* When have you really had to knuckle down and make things happen? Were there times when you kept going when everything else seems to be going against you? How many times have you failed at something – anything – and you've tried and tried again until success came your way? *(Persistence, motivation, drive, resilience.)* What changes have you dealt with in your life; if you've driven them yourself how have you tapped into your drive and energy and passion to make them happen? If they happened outside your control, how did you handle them? *(Resilience, ability to cope with change).* What negative experiences have you been through that you've learnt from? How could you show a stranger the person you truly are, as opposed to a bunch of qualifications listed neatly on a page? *(That's written communication, persuading, influencing, expressing.)* What sort of person would they see? It's these qualities that you need to bring out in your CV or interviews when applying for jobs or courses. *(That's self-promotion.)*

It's also about those things which prompted you to make the choices you have in work, play and leisure, and in the friends you hang around with. *(That shows what motivates you.)* What circumstances have you grown up in which have influenced you, your actions, your choices and the messages you've taken on board about yourself, life, the opportunities ahead? *(Decision making and action planning skills here.)* What have you done to challenge them? *(You don't settle for just anything!)* What have you done to help yourself? These sorts of things have all contributed to make up the person you are by influencing and moulding you over the years. It will also show you that being successful – however you define success – takes tremendous hard graft, self-discipline and continual, sustained effort. Without ingredients such as these, success all too often feels hollow, empty and unsatisfying. Look at all the times you've been proactive and what the results were. Look at the opportunities you created for yourself by getting off your backside and making something happen. *(Taking the initiative.)* If you want to be successful in the way you envisage success, you need to do that again and again.

It's also about your professional and personal development as an engineer, inventor or creator, and how you untapped your creativity. Who or what has inspired you along the way? Can you discuss and debate the various merits of those key people working in the niche sector you want to get into, those from whom you've taken inspiration and courage. How do you tend to get your ideas and what happens from then on in? How can you show that you've worked with a team of people to bring an idea to fruition? Where do you pull your ideas from and how do you research an idea and the process along the way?

However, you've studied towards your degree, be it full time, part time or by distance learning, so congratulate yourself. Go out with a group of friends and sink a few drinks. But take time to quietly, independently and proudly assess what you've achieved and, crucially, the characteristics in your personality, the motivators and drivers which have empowered you to success, such as persistence, determination and curiosity. You've had the endurance to get through a degree, and developed the ability to network, form working relationships fast, to take responsibility for your own career development and learning and to be resourceful.

Acknowledge your strengths and resources in writing

Written down, they will give you a lift, especially if you're feeling low. Whatever stage of life you're at, you'll need to draw on all your resources to create the future you want. Get ready to dig deep and raise your energy levels, standards, focus, persistence and drive to a higher level to propel yourself into making it happen. Finally, you'll be able to tell employers more succinctly what lies behind the person you are – and the person you want to be, thereby selling yourself more effectively. Self-presentation and promotion is an important skill at work today.

The power of work experience

Work experience strengthens your hand in the employment market, particularly if it is targeted towards the career you intend to follow and structured in such a way that you can learn and put the theory you have learnt on your degree course into practice. Employers can see you in action for themselves: the way you walk and talk, think and act, behave and motivate, initiate and inspire, work and apply your new-found knowledge. They want to see how effective you are and how you achieve results. In fact, employers rate work experience and internships as a highly effective way to find graduate recruits. There are many schemes on offer throughout the year for varying periods of time. Their entry is often highly competitive, requiring the same professional approach and strategy to achieve success as job hunting.

The small and medium enterprise (SME) market in its own right can give you the chance to put your foot in the door. There may be a scheme running in your area to help companies and graduates benefit each other. The National Council for Work Experience has a lot more information on its website (www.work-experience. org). Also look for opportunities to gain experience through professional bodies and trade associations' websites. Check out STEP at www.step.org.uk which arranges placements with companies for a year or shorter periods of time. Many of the websites listed in this book have details of work placements, internships and residencies and you need to get to know which sites are most suitable for you. Internships and work experience placements are very competitive and it can be hard to survive for three months with just your travel expenses. However, it is an excellent way in, so consider it as an investment, just as your university studies are.

You don't have to sign up for a specific scheme. You could approach a company directly for experience, which may be a great way to get into a smaller company that may not be aware of opportunities to join placement schemes. Keep trying and persisting.

1 Identify what it is that you need to practise at work – are there particular skills you want to use?
2 Pinpoint what you will bring to the employer – enthusiasm and a passion for what you're doing are a start.
3 Give the employer examples of what you can do and what you would like to do, so that he has a menu of choices.
4 Show him what you have done so far, so that he has a clear idea of what you're capable of.
5 Give an allotted time-scale but be flexible.
6 Find out if the company has a project which needs to be done which no-one else has time to do.
7 Ask for an assessment of your work at the end, so that the employer can write a testimonial and you can together work out what you have achieved and got out of the placement.

Work experience should play a central role in your sales strategy when you start job hunting. It shows that you know what you're letting yourself in for. You can talk about your experiences and achievements at interview and demonstrate your effectiveness through the job-specific and transferable skills you've used. You can prove how you can be relied on to get results, to make things happen and to achieve. You can prove your passion for, and belief in, what you're doing, that you've got your hands dirty. Talk the lingo, understand the frustrations, challenges, issues, opportunities and threats. As a rule, the longer and more relevant the experience, the more beneficial it will be.

If you've found a work experience on your own, turn it into a constructive learning time. Identify what you want out of it and what you have to offer before you approach an employer. Find out if there is a project you can do to practise specific skills and put your course theory into practice. Observe closely and ask the right questions and you'll acquire an insight into how the different parts of the organisation pull together as everyone works to fulfil the mission or vision set out in its profile.

You can pick up the language relevant to the sector and the organisation or company itself. You can pick up business lingo relevant to the business world with terms such as 'profit and loss', 'added value', 'key performance indicators', and you will understand what they are. Listening skills are important if you're to pick up the language and way of working specific to the business. Each one has its own terminology relating to its systems, protocol, meetings, hierarchy, and many have their own intranet. Work experience gives you insight into how companies function and helps you make those all-important contacts. *'I've got a friend who works in PR. Shall I mention you to her? She could give you a call for a chat.'*

Finally, remember that working at the bottom of the organisation is a great way to learn how the various parts work, who the key decision makers are, and why the bottom line is so important.

Work to close any skills gaps

Every industry has its problems recruiting staff with the right skills. In many niche areas, there are cluster groups, forums and groups of employers, industry specialists and training providers who are trying to tackle the problem and encourage employers to offer (graduates) a way in and a structured learning environment. Ideas which are being developed include apprenticeship programmes, business realisation schemes, training programmes and career-entry initiatives. Go to the heart of the industry to find out what is being undertaken in yours. Professional bodies and the various sector skills councils will tell you more.

Meantime, why not show someone who works in the sector a copy of your CV and ask them where your skills gaps are? How can you go about closing them? It may be that a short training programme will do the trick, or perhaps a stint of work experience with exposure to a particular area will help.

What behaviours and practices do you need to elicit to make your 'it' happen?

- Be very determined. Push for your corner, but remain polite.
- Get focused.
- Be prepared to sacrifice something else in your life so that you can give what you really want the hours it deserves. True friends will understand if you can only meet them once a fortnight or once a week.

Go out there and start building up your portfolio of projects to demonstrate your 'can do' approach

Here are some ideas:

1   Get out there on site at every opportunity you have to acquire a clear understanding of how site and office work together. Can you get a day a week with a local company working on the area you wish to work in or start working for them part time while studying? Work experience schemes can be highly competitive but this could be a great way 'in' to put your theory into practice.

2   While you're looking for the right opportunity, build up a portfolio by doing things for yourself, working on projects and ideas in the area you want to get into.

3   Use your network, formal and informal, to promote yourself. It just needs one person to mention it in the right place at the right time.

4   Get your work out there where it can be seen, at shows, exhibitions, trade events, student presentations and professional bodies' groups.

5   Look for a problem in society and find a way to solve it using your creativity and technical expertise. Why not approach the task with another graduate whose skills complement yours? Investigate the funding available for any ideas you have from governments, universities, research outlets, trusts – any possible group you can think of.

6   Could you work with your university to take an idea, turn it into a commodity and turn in into a spin-out company? Or is

there the opportunity to join one with current staff members as an assistant or researcher and developer?

7   Can you find out your idea's market value? What would it cost to produce and what sort of profit could you be talking about? Talk business savvy, with potential markets, think about the how, when and where you would take the product or your service to market.

8   Take part in competitions, exhibitions and awards, either as an observer, a visitor or an entrant and competitor.

9   Get used to competing. You will need to compete and pitch for business so get used to the adrenalin buzz of doing so. Find ways to boost your performance.

Get out on site so that you get the feel of how all the different elements of design, engineering and construction link together in the most practical sense.

Draw up a year planner

1   Undertake a complete search of all the shows, exhibitions, awards and competitions you wish to enter as an exhibitor (which will mean preparing something to display) or attend as a visitor (which will mean identifying what you want to get out of the visit prior to the event). Put them on a wall planner, along with any other known commitments such as deadlines for course assignments, projects, job application deadlines, exams, your graduation day, key social and family dates, and anything else which comes to mind.

2   Of those shows you plan to attend as an exhibitor, if this is your first show, how much information can you glean from the show organisers and the material they send out about the event? Many events have a list of exhibitors up on their websites prior to the show, enabling you to make contact with exhibitors you'd like to meet to arrange a chat during the show. Why not contact some of the people who attended as exhibitors last year to see what advice they have for you as a new entrant? Can you arrange to meet them there for a coffee to ask their advice or use the event as a way to secure an introduction to ask for help?

3   Plan how long it will take to prepare for the events if you're going to exhibit at them. If you are unsure, ask a more expe-

rienced show entrant, such as a past winner. What exactly do you need to do to put on the best showing you can? Apart from any products and designs, this may include preparing marketing material about yourself, such as your CV (up-to-date), a business card, a CD showing your work and giving CV details and even a website you can refer people to.

4   How important is each event to you and your career? What else is likely to be featuring in your life at the time and in the weeks ahead which may be competing for your time, energy and attention? How can you organise yourself so that you really are at your best for what is most important to you? Can you talk to those important to you in your life to ask for their particular support and understanding in the weeks leading up to the event?

5   What exactly do you want from each show – Contacts? Work? Commissions? Who else will be there that you could make sure you make contact with? What price you will be charging for work you get? Who can help you with this advice – Tutors? Professional bodies? Are you prepared to handle any approaches made to you for your work from a mental, practical and business point of view?

6   Allow time after the event to follow through any work you need to do, such as following up contacts and handling requests for information about you and your work, capitalising on any positives such as wins or offers of work. Can you send an article back to your home town newspaper, for example 'Local Student Wins Award!' or go on a local radio show? Check the Newspaper Society at www.newspapersoc.org.uk/ or worldwide at http://www.wrx.zen.co.uk/alltnews.htm for lists of your local papers. Be your own PR manager.

Start behaving and immersing yourself in the field you want to be in

If you're job hunting, devote full-time effort to the task. Keep your ambitions and goals at the forefront of your mind, or they will lose their prominence in your heart and it will take more effort to make them happen, especially if you consider yourself to be in a 'lower level' role right now. Position yourself to get out of it, either by moving or staying put, or one of two things can happen, as shown in Figure 6.3.

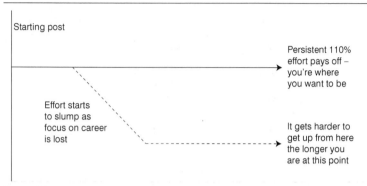

Figure 6.3

Think about projects you've done which will be relevant to potential employers

Make sure you're ready to talk to potential employers about projects you've done.

- What did you do to make them happen on your own and in a group?
- What was the scale of the project?
- How did you turn that idea into a commercial opportunity?
- What could its potential be? How could it impact on the community and the wider world? Who would the stakeholders be?
- What would the cost be? Who would be involved in the financing? Who would you have dealt with to acquire the financing?
- What applications did you use? What technology? Be prepared to talk about the what, how and at what stage you used it.

Network, network, network

Take the wheel of networking in Figure 6.4. At some time in your life, you may focus on one segment more than others; you may want to add or delete a segment. Aim for a balanced wheel, so that you can tap into the support you need for a healthy, balanced life and successful, happy career. Tap into every corner to see if any (albeit unexpectedly) can provide you with the opportunity you need to truly kick off your career and life in the direction you want it to go.

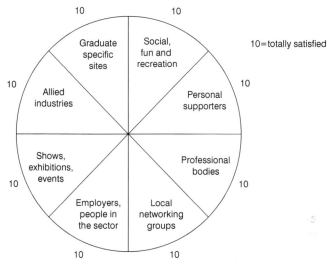

Figure 6.4

1   What are you doing to make something happen in each segment to create the career and life you want?

2   Which do you need to focus on *more* to get the results you need and make the connections you want?

3   Which section(s) should the *hub* of your network be at right now so that you can tackle the most important and urgent issues in your life?

4   How much activity do you have in it or them at the moment? How much time are you spending on accessing them and getting yourself known? How often are you making new contacts in it? Which is yielding the best results?

5   What do you need to do to make sure the sector you need to have the strongest network in is up to par to get the results you need in your life?

Short-term solutions to long-term challenges

Work experience and temporary assignments or contract work all give you the opportunity to show what you can do. They may lead to a permanent role. This is particularly the case if you want to switch from your degree subject and go into an area which you know little about or consider your options. They enable you to show what you can do. During your holidays, investigate what is possible with companies which you would give your right arm to join.

People temp for many reasons. You could do it to give yourself time to decide what to do, using its flexibility to build your portfolio, making contacts, getting a foot in the door of the industry you want to work in. You can also use it to pick up lots of ideas for your own business, watching how businesses do things, considering how design can help companies grow or not and help people work more effectively together. It can be helpful to sharpen up your business skills and approach and give the way you handle your own affairs a more professional and crisper image.

Temporary work offers flexibility but it does not guarantee you a regular income. The time you spend worrying about whether you'll have work next week may well be better devoted to your craft. It will, however, put you right into the heart of the workplace, enabling you to build up a web of contacts around a number of companies. You'll quickly find that you're not the only one doing a day job and then getting home to focus on their main job. On the other hand, temping may enable you to take a week off (unpaid) to prepare for that exhibition. If you take this route, you'll need to be able to cope well with uncertainty and swift changes to your day.

If you choose to temp through an agency, remember that first and foremost they are businesses seeking to make a profit, so take responsibility for plotting and planning your own career. Whatever reason you temp for, keep your eye on the goal you're aiming for. The *danger* of temping is that you could still find yourself temping after a year, with no further progress in your decision making. Don't allow your own ambitions and aspirations to get lost in the process.

Five steps to getting 'in' to a company through temping

1   Hook up with a specialist agency which focuses on the specific sector you want to work in. If you're still thinking about what you want to do and you're thinking that it's not relating to your degree, sign up with a high street name which covers many sectors to broaden your insight and experience. A visit to the company's website will help you assess its strengths and focus and track record.

2   When you sign up with an agency, dress as if you're going for an interview so that the agency knows it can send you out with confidence. Your consultant should talk through your skills, competencies and career goals. Ask how often and by what method you should keep in touch. Check emails and your mobile regularly for messages. Try to get two, three-week or month assignments together in one sector to enhance your CV's consistency. Be more flexible at first and show you can be trusted first before you get choosey.

3   Look for ways to put the knowledge and skills you've acquired through your university experience into practice in the company you're with. Ask the company for projects or you can do them voluntarily to help develop your skills.

4   Reflect weekly on skills and knowledge you're acquiring. Which environments have you thrived most in? What have you achieved? Get feedback from your agency and the company you're with.

5   Update your CV regularly and ensure the agency has a copy so that they can send out your most recent one. Focus on your transferable skills and consider exactly how they will help the sector you want to join.

6   Consider what you need to start doing to make the overall experience more effective and to take you closer to achieving your goals. What strategies can you employ to make these happen?

Many people find work exhausting enough without doing career planning back home too. But this is where 110 per cent commitment and effort will get you to where you want to be, while the 90 per cent won't, so raise your standard.

How do you take time out to go for interviews while you're working?

Companies are paying for you to be there and do the job they need you to do, not to keep disappearing for interviews with others – who may be their competitors. If you keep calling in sick, this makes you look unreliable in the eyes of the agency *and* employer. Many companies will interview people first thing in the morning or late afternoon. Work extra hours the day before or after at your temporary assignment. Give your (temporary) employer as much notice as possible. Work at 110 per cent and they won't want to lose you. Ask your agency for advice as to how to best handle the situation.

Don't wait for doors to open for you. Get out there and start knocking on doors to connect to the opportunities you want.

Learn from others you deem to be successful – how do they do it?

Seek out those who are where you wish to be. They've done it. But *how did they get there?* People love to talk about themselves and many will see it as a compliment if you ask their advice. If they see passion and enthusiasm in you, they'll be more than happy to help.

Go to the major shows and exhibitions and talk to the exhibitors. How did they get to where they are today? What advice would they have for you? What has their career path been and what are the three most important factors which have contributed to their success? Contact people at the top of their companies and careers or the winners of awards and exhibitions. Well, why not? What lessons have they learnt along the way that they can pass on to you? Follow up major show winners with an email to congratulate them and then ask their advice. Read Sarah Brown's book, *Moving on up*, with advice and stories from leaders in many sectors on how they got to the top and what it takes.

Get ahead – get a mentor

Mentors have been there, done it and got the t-shirt. They can be an invaluable source of help, advice and contacts and many mentors get a great deal from the process themselves. A mentor will talk to you about your goals aspirations and how you can get there. They will help you stay on track and keep focused. There are lots of mentor programmes available though many specialist networking groups and you should look at various websites listed throughout this book to find one which suits your needs. Mentoring can be done face-to-face or over the telephone. If you want to get ahead, learn from those who will make you think about what you're doing, asking you questions which you wouldn't think of asking yourself.

Heading for self-employment or want to develop your business acumen?

Consider these questions:

* Name three companies which are success stories (they can be any size)?
* What makes them successful?
* What works well for them? What doesn't?
* What makes customers and clients turn to them for products and services?
* What can you learn from them and apply to your own business?

Now let's do this exercise differently:

* Name three companies which have not been successful or which are going through a really rough time.
* Where are they going wrong?
* What are they trying to do to put things right?
* What has put customers and clients off them for products and services?
* What can you learn from them and apply to your own business?

Brainstorm with friends or join forces with other graduates to see what you can learn from them and their outlook.

Be sure you are truly aware of all the support available to you, both as a graduate and in the sector you wish to work in.

Summary action points

Turn your experience from an academic one into a work-related one which means something to employers and gets you in the right mind-set.

1   Look to see how you can start living the working day so far as possible.

2   Identify steps you can take which will bring you closer to the role you want.

3   Review your progress to date in areas such as: your own self-awareness and how far that has come; your picture of your career and life in the next three to five years; how your network has changed; and how far you've researched potential employers (or courses) to apply to.

4   How can you change your behaviour to get the success you want? What could you do differently?

Chapter 7

Promoting and selling yourself

The next stage, as you prepare to sell yourself, is to consider questions such as:

- ◆ What is most relevant in your life history for you to tell recruiters about when you consider the opportunities you seek?
- ◆ What can you do to boost your chances of success?
- ◆ What can you control? What is outside your control? (For example, you can control the time you spend job hunting and where you choose to job hunt.)

If you respond to an advert in a newspaper, you *can* control the quality of your application, but you *cannot* control the numbers of applicants applying for the same post. You can choose to demonstrate your ability to communicate clearly and present your case well by submitting a well thought out, easily read and well expressed application.

Remember, enlist several ways of job hunting – don't put all your eggs into one basket. Aim to do something with each method at least once a week.

Once you've identified a vacancy or course you would like to take or an employer you would like to work for:

1 Identify any deadlines so that you can work out what to do and when, and pinpoint what needs to be done;

2 Assess the skills, knowledge, acumen and attitude your potential employer needs by researching their organisation carefully;

3   Identify the evidence you need to paint the picture of your
     capabilities and aspirations from your research, life resources,
     characteristics to date, work experience, voluntary work, trav-
     el, leisure, team efforts and projects.

4   If you need to include a CV with your application, write it out
     until you are comfortable with it; produce a one-page letter of
     application and anything else required. In your one-page letter,
     highlight the skills and experience you have which are relevant
     to the role you are applying for, and explain why the company
     you are writing to appeals to you. Mention something about
     the company which shows you know a bit about them – per-
     haps a recent campaign they've designed for a client.

5   Before you submit your application, have it checked by some-
     one else and copy it, so that you can refer to it before inter-
     view.

To save time, understand how companies recruit

If you are applying to a small company (50 people or less), the way
to apply may be by sending a carefully thought through and well
presented letter of application, together with a CD of your portfolio and your CV to the boss. Spell out what your qualifications
mean to make life easy for them. Get rid of any educational jargon.
Large companies will probably have a recruitment process that includes application forms, personality tests, telephone interviews, assessment centres, interviews and more, all organised by a graduate
recruitment section.

If you have to complete an application form, and send a CV with
it, it is tempting to put 'see CV' on many answers, which in itself
could lead to your application being deleted. Application forms give
recruiters an opportunity to compare applicants, so apply the 110
per cent effort rule as opposed to 80 per cent. This rule also needs
to be applied persistently and with rigour throughout the job hunting process. Remember that natural good manners can set you apart
from other candidates throughout the process. No-one wants to recruit someone who is rude, surly and sulky.

Submit an outstanding application, not just an excellent one

In the recruitment process, there is one winner, i.e. the person who is selected, who will stand out over the other applicants. The person who is selected will have probably given an outstanding performance from start to finish; the others may all be excellent, but in a competitive world, there is only one winner. So if you're going to put yourself a cut above all the other applicants, you need to make yourself stand out as an outstanding candidate.

Get physical

It's a competitive world out there, so prepare yourself to fight for your part in it. Exercise daily to sharpen your mind and body – the results will be apparent from your added energy and increased focus. Minimise the rubbish you eat and drink, including alcohol. Mental agility exercises will help you improve your ability to think on your feet.

Put yourself in the recruiter's shoes

Think about what you know about the company and the sector, and the role they are recruiting for. What are they looking for? What do they want? There are plenty of specialist books regarding CVs, application forms, applying online, assessment centres and the interview process and these are all listed under Further Information at the end of this book. Raise your standard over all the other candidates: invest a few hours in a good read. In addition, many agencies have hints and advice on their websites, so make the most of it.

Get practice in tests

If you know tests will form part of the assessment, ask your careers service for a practice run. Know what you're letting yourself in for; get used to handling questions, managing your time, and focusing on a task. The website www.prospects.ac.uk enables you to get your CV checked, talk to graduate employers and practice online personality and aptitude tests.

Six golden rules to kick off

1   Use a professional email address, putting your contact details at the bottom and use an appropriate header in the subject box, such as Graduate Opportunities. Address it to the right person; check their name on the company's website or by calling the switchboard.

2   Check your mobile and email regularly for messages. Recruitment can move quickly.

3   Where you are responding to an advertisement for a post and there is a reference number, give it in your letter of application or email subject header.

4   Make your application easy for recruiters to read; use bullet points, not prose. Explain your educational qualifications – spell out subjects you covered and the skills you've acquired.

5   On your CV, use a short opening statement of 30–40 words to describe your career aspirations, relating them to the role you're applying for or the company you'd like to work for. Describe the person who lies behind the CV or application form through your use of adjectives.

6   Paint the reader a picture of the scale of the projects or achievements you've worked on, using numbers, targets, deadlines, results, feedback and percentages. This will demonstrate your personal effectiveness in getting results. If your degree grants you exemptions to certain professional qualifications, say so. Be specific about the technology and computer applications you can use.

Business acumen, creativity and innovation are key aspects many employers will be looking for. They'll want customer focus, ideas, solutions to problems and challenges, and energy, drive, ambition and hunger to get things done and done correctly. Can you show that you've brought ideas to the table before and made them happen? Figure 7.1 below shows some of the features you need to think about.

Many employers are bored with the thousands of applications coming through their door all looking the same, sounding the same, feeling the same, talking about the same skills, abilities, etc. They are often looking for that something that makes them say '*Wow, I'd like to meet this person*'. It can be one simple line or sentence.

Are you heading for any of the following?		Obtain evidence of your
• Employment • Work experience • Internship • Further study • Initiatives such as Knowledge Transfer Partnerships • Post-graduate course • Short training course	*To sell yourself succesfully, you will need to show that you've got what they need*	• Passions and interests • Values and motivation • Ability to contribute to their success • Skills: transferable and job-specific • Experience • Technical expertise • Research you've done into the sector • An understanding of what it's like to work and be at work • Something that grabs their attention and makes you stand out

Figure 7.1

While studying for your degree, you'll have learnt a range of skills, which may include:

+ Numeracy
+ Different approaches to problem solving
+ Project management
+ Flexibility
+ Creativity
+ Interpreting drawings and measurements
+ Team working
+ Organising projects, materials, people, timescales
+ Commercial acumen – watching that bottom line
+ Health and safety.

The application process gives you the opportunity to highlight these skills.

Make CVs personal and relevant to the company you're writing to

A CV should include headings for areas such as:

+ Contact details (at the very top, easily spotted);
+ Academic history (most recent first), pinpointing the most relevant modules of your course to the employer and mentioning any exemptions from professional qualifications the course has given you, if relevant;

- Relevant work experience and employment history with dates and job titles. Outlines of projects you have worked on, the size of each company you worked for, and the skills you used, including managerial experience. Talk in terms of size and costs and achievements, e.g. project completed in time and on budget. Outline the skills you used which will be relevant to the recruiter reading your CV;
- Overall achievements and positions of responsibility;
- Interests and leisure – keep it brief and honest;
- Personal details – for example, '*Willing to re-locate*' if you are; a clean driving licence; nationality and age (put date of birth as opposed to age in years);
- Technical knowledge, especially if the employer has stated a need for the successful applicant to have it. If you are sending out unsolicited CVs, give the full range of technical expertise you have.

Pay particular attention to the way you lay out your CV, from the font size and type to the layout and way you organise the information you wish to portray. Keep it simple, but make it look good. Limit your CV to two sides or less, and use one font type and colour. Send it by email or by post on paper (good quality white A4 with no gimmicks, designs, wrinkles or coffee stains). Don't put 'Curriculum Vitae' at the top – employers know what it is. Consider the sector you want to work in. Some, such as the professions – accountancy, banking, law, etc. – expect conventional CVs. Others, such as the media, expect candidates to be more creative with attention to layout and typescript, but not pretentious.

As you move further up the career ladder, put more emphasis on your employment history than on your educational qualifications and work experience, and select the two or three responsibilities and achievements from each role which most closely match the role you want. You will need to talk more about the overall impact you had on the company from a wider viewpoint.

Many applications are wasted because they are riddled with spelling errors, hard to read and poorly researched. Others get a glance and perhaps go into a 'think about while reading the rest' pile. Some are easy to read and relevant, and then one or two will make the employer sit up and take notice. You want your CV to be in that one or two.

They want one year's experience

If you were to add up all your work experience and put it together on your CV, you may be surprised to find that it adds up to close to a year. Can you add to that paid and unpaid experience, commissions, contracts, work simulated projects, and voluntary efforts? Put all your work experience together in a CV and put it first before your educational qualifications so that it draws the employer's attention before anything else.

Outline the projects and subjects you have worked on to date

If you have had a number of these, choose the ones which you think are most relevant to the role you now want. Give information which shows the scale of your achievements to a potential employer, giving names, dates, and details of the work involved. If you have a website, refer the employer to it. There you can include a brief description of each work, but not too much – you want them to be hungry enough to find out more about the person behind the ideas and pieces they see.

What happens after submitting your application?

As said before, for the small or medium-sized employer, you will probably need to send a CV and accompanying letter of application and then attend for an interview.

For larger firms, kick-off may involve sending in your CV or completing an online or paper application form, or perhaps doing an online psychometric test or personality questionnaire. Many employers then run initial screening by way of short telephone interviews with candidates. Regardless of who you're applying to, ask your housemates to answer the phone with greater courtesy than usual; explain that you're job hunting. Keep your details, a pen and paper by the phone, with a generic CV with your life history on it so you can quickly refer to grades you've obtained, if asked, or find information required.

Look at your potential: where do you want to be?

Where do you see yourself in five years' time? Who *do you want to become?* Increasingly, job prospects relate to the person you are and want to become (your potential), hence the heavy emphasis on psychological tests, assessment centres and even handwriting analysis in the recruitment process. It is not a good idea to say *'I'd like to be running my own company'* or *'I'll be travelling on a year off'* or *'I'd like to be in your job'.* Show ambition, but not at the expense of the interviewer, unless you're applying to a large company where there are clear ladders of progression. An employer will also want to know that you're a stayer. The recruitment process is a long and costly one, so they won't want to take on somebody who intends to leave within a year plus of joining, unless you move up their ranks.

This is a question that employers like to ask when recruiting and many job hunters think, *'Wow. I don't even know where I want to be next week! Why are these guys so hooked on this question?'* The thing to remember is that recruiting and training staff cost money and time and it's a risk. Employers need to know where your level of ambitions and drive are taking you, what your values and aspirations are and where you see yourself going. They need to look at the staff they are recruiting, to assess the spread of talents and skills they need and how you might fit and contribute to fulfilling their long-term vision, now and in the future. Large global organisations, for example, may have had to forecast their recruitment needs over a year ago. But many companies also recruit as the need arises, particularly if they small, asking *'What could this person do for us starting from Monday?'* on the one hand, and wanting people who can grow with and contribute to the organisation on the other.

The fact that you have a degree shows your commitment to learning and developing yourself and realising your potential. An employer can see that by evidence of your conscious decision to study for a degree. They know you have the ability to learn and juggle life, study and work and progress. They can build on your strengths, weaknesses, skills, creativity, leadership abilities and management material. They can train you, probably promote you, give you a team of people to manage and expect results from you. They may provide financial and timely support for you to study towards professional examinations but they need to know that you can and will stand the pace of working relatively long hours during the weekday and studying at night. They'll look for the evidence in your application from start to finish.

More importantly, you and any potential employer need to know that you're right for each other. This is very much a two-way process. If you are not right for each other, it's far better to acknowledge it immediately. The way the organisation is structured may not enable you to meet your aspirations. Equally, if you're going on to further study, make sure the thing you are applying for, be it a course or role, is right for you and your long-term plans.

Interestingly, this also applies if you want to set up your own business – know where you are and where you're going, and you're more likely to get there.

Post-graduate? Consider the difference …

If you're a post-graduate, stand back and look at yourself from the time you completed your undergraduate degree and your post-graduate degree. Assess the difference the two made to you personally; what has changed about you and your approach as a result of your post-graduate studies? What particular skills, knowledge and breadth have you acquired from the second degree and how would that make a difference to an employer? What difference has it made to your character and personality, your strength, direction and self-belief? How can you sell those effectively to make a living from them or market them to employers? How can you show employers that you have extra fine tuned skills in analytical thinking, communication, self-management and motivation and in the way you look at how things are done and how other people think, work and do things? Many students find that employers treat them the same as their undergraduate peers but, as the post-graduate, it is for you to take responsibility and make sure that your input and contribution is over and above what is expected of you.

Prepare to show your commercial awareness

Continue to research the sector you want to work in: industry news, who are the movers and shakers, who's who and which companies work in it. What sort of pressures are companies under? Where does the company fit into the sector and how does it stand out from its competitors? Why do they appeal to you over their competitors?

Can you talk about their products and services, their culture and ethos. How did they start and what has their growth been like? You want to join a company which is in the ascendent, not one which is spluttering and faltering, and starting to gasp for breath. Who are their main clients or customers and what have their recent campaigns, products and services been? What are the hot topics and issues of the day, and who is in the news and for what? Check share prices and read the last couple of annual reports to see how far the company is moving towards achieving its goals or vision. Pick up on the bigger picture by researching the company through the Internet and printed press, and talking to people who may know about it. Demonstrate you understand how organisations are organised and function. Your one-page covering letter of application can make a good start in showing this off as you outline why you chose to apply to the company over its competitors.

Show how you can benefit the company and fit in

Demonstrate that you have researched these points:

- What is the company's mission and vision?
- How does it expect to achieve that?
- What will it need to achieve it?
- What sort of drive and personal qualities from its employees will it need to be successful?
- What can you contribute to the organisation as it works to achieve its vision?
- What does the consumer/client want?
- What are the trends and challenges facing the sector?
- What qualities will they be looking for in their employees? How can you demonstrate that you have them?
- What specific job skills does the recruiter call for that you can prove you have?
- What can you bring to the team that might be an added dimension?
- Are you ready to answer competency-based questions, with specific examples and to work through them in detail, giving employers a clear picture of how you approach problems and processes?

- Can you show that if they sponsor you for a professional qualification or a post-graduate course, that you'll commit to it in its entirety?

Each boss or line-manager has their own criteria to meet as they recruit for a role. These may refer to particular skills which are essential to the job, such as particular IT packages, and will assess every application throughout against these criteria; they may ask the same questions of all candidates to compare their answers. There may be someone from human resources there to check any legal requirements, to ensure that the other interviewers remain on track and ask appropriate questions, and to cover company benefits. Your prospective boss will look at your skills set and how they will fit with his requirements and, crucially, how you will fit in with the team. If you're applying for a small company, the boss and a member of the team may fulfil both roles.

Personal fit with the team

Well, you either fit, or you don't. And if you don't, it is more to do with the existing team as it is and the sort of person the selectors are looking to add to it. For this reason, you may be called back for several interviews with different members of the team to build up an all-round view of how you're going to fit in. View it each time as an opportunity to take a closer look at your potential colleagues. What would it be like arriving for work every day first thing in the morning and making small talk by the coffee machine? It is essential to be yourself throughout the process if this fit is to be right, real and genuine, so welcome each opportunity. Your colleagues will want to feel comfortable working with you on an assignment until three in the morning, and you'll want to feel good working alongside them.

Go into the recruitment process prepared to have fun

Most recruiters want to give you a good experience – they know you'll tell friends and family on what you thought of them. They know that if you are not in a situation where you can be yourself, they won't see the true you. The truth is that recruiters have a responsibility to take the right people on for the right roles, which is no easy task. Be prepared for the interviewer whose technique is appalling – rambling, non-stop, rude and arrogant. The website www. doctorjob.com can tell you more.

The assessment centre

Many (larger) companies use assessment centres to select their new recruits, lasting a morning or more to see how you'll cope with the demands and stresses of the job. They'll include activities such as team tasks and activities, numeracy and written tests, role-related tests (for example, creating an advert for a product if you were going into advertising), interviews and presentations, and company-specific tests. Look at each exercise from the employer's point of view. What competence or quality do you think they are looking for in the tests they have included? Focus on each one as it appears. Be prepared for the unexpected. You may be asked to present on a subject unknown to you, so that the selectors can see how you handle presenting, debating and working under pressure. Social events may not 'count' towards the assessment, but you'll be quietly watched to see how you interact. Find out what makes your potential work colleagues tick – will you want to be working with them every day under pressure? Drink an absolute minimum of alcohol. You want to be 110 per cent the next day while everyone else is at 80–90 per cent.

Attending an interview

If you decide to do freelance and contract work, you will need to sell yourself continually, so 'selling yourself' meetings and interviews will become second nature to you. That said, some nerves are a good sign – they show you care. But whether self-employed or job-hunting, preparing for an interview or assessment day takes place at several levels:

* Reviewing what you know about the sector you want to work in and the professional career you've chosen to follow (if relevant);
* Researching the company using every possible resource available to you. Visit any local stores or branches. Obtain brochures and read them carefully. What impression do they give you of the company? How comfortable would you feel having

the staff there as colleagues? What recent projects have they worked on and what do you know about them?

- Reminding yourself of what you can contribute to that company and how it matches your career goals;
- Practical preparations, such as dressing the part, getting there with time to spare;
- Preparing mentally for questions you may be asked, such as *What are your strengths? Tell us about a team effort you've contributed to and what your role was. Tell us about yourself!*
- Preparing the night before – have an early night, keep alcohol to a minimum and don't eat anything with a strong flavour such as garlic.

Getting yourself in the right frame of mind. There's no point in taking baggage that spells the *'Oh poor me, I'll never get a job'* feeling. Leave it at home, put some music on which makes you feel really great en route, and focus on the task ahead. Remember, this interview is a two-way process and a chance for you to ensure that this employer is right for you, just as they need to make sure you're right for them.

A word about the *'Tell us about yourself'* question. This is not an invitation for you to recite your entire life history. Outline in a couple of sentences where you are now and where you want to be. Keep it short and throw them a couple of points they can pick up on.

Dress the part

Review your appearance. Is there anything you need to do, such as:

- Polishing shoes
- Getting shoes re-heeled
- Cleaning under your nails
- Getting a hair cut
- Making sure your suit isn't too tight or skirt too short
- Deciding what you could wear if you had to 'perform' two days running
- Looking for accessories which would enhance your image
- Not overdoing make-up, perfume or aftershave
- De-cluttering your handbag, so that you can find items easily in it

* Making sure your writing equipment – a pen and notebook – is easy to carry, professional, that your pen works and you have a standby.

Take along a copy of your CV, questions you have to ask, and any research you've found. Take directions of how to get there, and contact details of the person who organised the interview, in case you run into a problem en route. Charge your mobile phone. Account for potential problems on route when planning your journey times.

What sort of questions should you expect?

* Why us?
  Be positive! Select two or three points which made them stand out against their competitors.
* What did you think of ...e.g. our brochure, website?
  Be able to back up your views. Can you compare the product or service with those of the competitors in the sector?
* What do you think you'll be doing in the first year?
  Comment on the research you've done through talking with other graduates and check your understanding of that role.
  Use the opportunity to ask questions you may have about that first year and your likely career progression.
* What is your perception of yourself?
  This is all about how you think you present yourself to people. They may ask you how you think you present yourself to them. How do you want to appear?
* What achievement are you proudest of?
  Think up several achievements before you go in and be prepared to talk about the work you put into making them so.
* What salary are you expecting?
  Outline the research you've done into salaries in the sector, both for new graduates and the industry as a whole. Be prepared to negotiate and remember that the added perks can affect the overall package considerably.

Remember, you're a graduate. On each point, show you've done your research and back up your answers with well thought out and cohesive answers which are clearly expressed. And be prepared to talk about techical subjects – an employer will want to test your application of knowledge, especially in areas relevant to your interests and the positions you're applying for, and to talk about projects you've done.

Questions to ask the interviewers

Ask questions which will enable you to build up a picture of what sort of relationship you're likely to have with this employer and how your working day and week might look, both upon joining, six months after joining and then in about two to five years' time.

- Is this a new position? If not, what is happening to the current post-holder? If the current post-holder is moving up or sideways, that's a signal of career progression; if the post is new, why has it been created? You need to ensure you're applying for a position which really *is* needed and has been thought through.
- Ask about the direction the company is taking – and how the company sees this post contributing to it.
- What training and career development will be available to you?
- Find out how long the interview process will take.

Be very clear about what you need to do to qualify and get the professional status you need

Before you sign on the dotted line, you need to make sure your employer will help you to achieve your professional qualifications and status. Some areas – such as RIBA's Professional Experience and Development Record Scheme, or PEDR – demand registration. Visit the website www.pedr.co.uk for more information.

Read the information available; make careful notes; ask for help where you need it. It may be helpful to draw a time-line for what you expect to happen when over the next few years. Mind map or list the areas you need to cover and work out with your employer exactly how you're going to ensure they happen and that you get the exposure you need to the experiences and projects required to make your professional status come into being. If you are not able to cover some areas, be creative and work through various options with your professional body's agreement. Discuss them with the careers advisers. Perhaps you could get the experience you need by working on projects abroad or by volunteering.

Whatever you do, be yourself

It is exhausting to keep up any pretence, and since both you and the company are trying to find out whether the two of you are suited to one another, it is also pointless. If you rapidly come to the conclusion that this company is not for you, then look at that as a positive. Have fun. Welcome the opportunity to test yourself, and be proud that you've got this far.

Offered the post!

Well done! Congratulations! Now, take a deep breath and consider the options ahead of you. Is this offer really what you want? Will you be happy walking into the organisation every Monday? Can you fulfil your short and longer-term career goals with it? Is the package right?

Add up perks and benefits

Perks vary, as employers provide increasingly individualised products and services for their employees, and much depends on size and sector, but Table 7.1 shows examples.

Table 7.1

Private healthcare	Joining bonus
Pension scheme	Personal accident insurance
Holidays	A sum of money to go towards a
Profit and performance related	course of the employee's choice
bonuses	Sharesave scheme
Buy or sell extra days holiday	Season ticket loan
Flexible working hours	Disability insurance
Child care discounts	Maternity and adoption phase-back
Discounted loans and mortgages	Summer shut down
Relocation packages	Company cars
Car lease schemes/discounts	Subsidised canteen
Financial support for professional	Language training
development	Sport and adventure training
Employee helpline	Insurance
Lifestyle managers	Travel cards
Pet insurance	Payment of professional association
Discretionary bonus	membership fees
Retirement plan	Work-wear
Social activities	

Perks and benefits all add up. Find out how your salary is likely to increase in the future. Bonuses will vary according to the industry you're in and how well your company – and/or you – perform. Find out what the salaries are in the industry via recruitment agencies and salary surveys. Look at the kind of positions you would expect to hold in say three or five years' time and see what the salaries and perks are for them. How different are they to what you currently earn?

Summary action points

Once you've started sending applications or taking steps towards your proposed first career move after your degree:

1   Keep a record of what you're sending out and when; this will help you to ascertain whether you're doing enough towards your goal.

2   Assess what is working particularly well and build on that.

3   Obtain feedback where you can to help you to improve your performance next time.

4   Get involved in a couple of things in life other than careers and job hunting to help keep a balance in your day and week.

Chapter 8

What's stopping you?
Make it happen!

Frequently in life, things seem to take far too long to go our way. We're waiting for that great job, or know that there isn't going to be one in the region we are in. We're waiting for a lucky break. But all too often, *we* are the people who stop ourselves getting what we want in life.

There are varying scenarios that befall us. For example, you can fall into a rut. You feel that you need a boost with the firepower of a space shuttle to get out of it, followed by a long sustained blast of persistent rocket fuel-type effort. This doesn't just happen in your career, but in relationships with people; perhaps the excitement has gone out of a relationship and you need a super-boost of impetus and excitement to bring it back to life. Perhaps your ability to be spontaneous in life has been overtaken by a preference for the known, safe and comfortable.

It may be that the situation you're in needs one bold, decisive step to get to where you want to be, but you feel like taking that step is like being asked to ski down the steepest, highest most icy slope. You just need to push yourself over the edge and set off, but it's making that first push which freezes you. At this point, we often fear failure and of looking like a fool in front of others – but we also fear success. We procrastinate from making that call, for fear of being turned down, rejected – but what if we succeed? How will we handle the changes in life that will invariably follow? Will we cope with them?

And then we make glorious plans, and life gets in the way. Family problems, a friend in trouble, illness, death, redundancy, changes thrust upon us, rows … they all combine to be the reasons why we are where we are.

And sometimes, it seems that we aren't getting anywhere or at least where we want to be as quickly as we wish. Maybe we're waiting for that magic breakthrough – selected at interview, obtaining funding for that post-graduate course, securing an introduction and follow up meeting with an employer you really want to work for, having a business idea in the shower. We're waiting, confident that these things will happen one day. If we don't stay on top of things and create the right environment and conditions for success, we will probably wait a long time.

It's at times like these that your university days can seem a distant memory, and the weight of debt around your neck heavier than ever.

Don't forget what you went to university for!

If your career plans are taking an age to come to fruition, it can be really frustrating to see all those successful people at work who didn't go to university who say, *'Well, university wasn't for me, and now I'm a millionaire several times over'*. It can be easy to fall into the trap of blaming others for your current situation, thinking and saying things like *'Well, the school pushed us into it'*, and *'My parents thought it would be a good idea'*.

Five survival tips are:

1   Recognise that there are gifted people who chose not go to university but who have made it up the ladder by another route – people reach their potential in their own way and time; what matters is that they get there.
2   Keep everything in perspective – you have as much chance of succeeding as they do.
3   Learn from them.
4   Recall what you got out of your university days. No one can ever take them away from you, or your degree.
5   Focus on where you want to be. Review the progress you've made so far and assess how far you've moved towards achieving your main goals. Identify what else you need to do.

Dig deeper into your resources

Whether you fall into a rut or you need to take that one decisive, courageous step, there will always be stages in your life where you need to get tough with yourself and dig deeper within you for the resources you need to achieve the result you want. These resources usually come from within us: energy, focus, clarity of vision and action required, determination, an ability to go out there and get on with it. You've done it before, when you chose to apply to university and then when you packed up and left home to head out there. It is *the* time to look afresh at the way you spend your time and energy and to get any unwanted stuff out of the way, such as anything that pulls you down.

Strengthen your resolve

You can choose to change your attitude, approach and luck, and you'll have subconsciously done so many times in your life when you felt good about what you were doing, things were going well, and you were on course for where you were heading. You may not have been aware that you were doing them. Since then, you probably picked up some bad habits, so it's a good time to make sure they aren't holding you back.

Dump the 'I'll try'. Trying isn't the answer

You can train yourself to think positively and talk positively by watching your language. If you're planning to do something, and think '*I'll try to do this before lunch tomorrow*', then in fact you're unlikely to do it. Think '*I will do this tomorrow before lunch*', and you inject a whole new energy into your focus and you're far more likely to get the thing done. Watch your language for a morning and listen for positive and negative statements. If you're talking more negatively than positively, that will be affecting your mood and manner. You can change that by simply talking more positively and changing your state and the way you're feeling.

What message are you taking on board?

Sometimes we don't help ourselves. If we're feeling down, and we watch a depressing television programme in which people are rowing and living mediocre lives, that's going to make us feel worse. If we listen to a piece of music we love and which makes us feel great and fantastic, then our approach to life changes. Aim for the positive and get a lift from it. Assess the information you receive in any format, dump the negative, work with the positive and strive for the possible and realistic.

Are you caught up in unhelpful patterns of thinking and behaviour?

Examples include criticising yourself, imposing limits or boundaries on the opportunities before you. It involves giving yourself excuses for failing before you start, spending more time on socialising than job hunting, so not giving your career the prominence in your life that it deserves. Perhaps you're being too influenced by listening to generalisations from people who don't know what they're talking about; or you're not applying any creativity to your problem to find a solution. Either way, you make the choice whether to take those on board and listen to them, or not.

Acknowledge there's a misunderstanding by others of what graduates can do for them

This is particularly the case in the SME market, where many bosses cannot keep up-to-date with all the changes in education at any level, unless they are parents. So make it easy for them. Pay particular attention to your work experience when you write your CV and paint as clear a picture as you can for them of what you can do with clear examples.

Use your problem-solving skills

What can you do to solve the problem?

1 Identify a problem or issue you have now, such as finding that first right role, making your business work, or paying off your student debts
2 Revise where you are now with the problem and identify the solution you want.
3 What is happening right now?
   ◆ What are you doing which is working for you?
   ◆ *You've tried everything?* Okay, ask yourself:
      ◆ What exactly have you tried?
      ◆ How often have you tried it?

- When specifically?
- How much time did you spend on it? How carefully did you do it?
- What is working well? What isn't?
- Look back over the last seven days. What did you do on each of those seven days to tackle the problem? If you only spent an hour on Monday and Wednesday doing something, you cannot expect to solve it.
- If you learn from this exercise that you're only spending two hours a week making new friends, but that friendship is important to you, then something in your week needs to change. You may need to sacrifice something else to allow room for the change to happen. If you want to work on your portfolio but only devote three hours a week to it, and four evenings to going out with friends, well, your social life is going to look pretty good; your portfolio won't. Devote four evenings to your portfolio, and that fifth evening spent with friends really will feel well deserved.

4 What extra resources and skills do you need to make the change happen? Table 8.1 gives hints!
5 Where will you get them from?
6 Look for new solutions.

- Brainstorm every single thing you can think of that you might do to change the situation to make it just the way you want it to be.
- What one thing do you need to do differently to get the results you need?
- What else could you do?
- What other ways could you approach the issue?
- What would you advise a friend to do?
- Who do you know who is where you want to be now?
- What help and advice could they offer you?

Table 8.1

Extra	Contacts
Skills	Knowledge
Time	Experience
Energy	Influence
Qualifications	Materials
Opportunities	

- Who might have experienced the same problem before and could help you unblock where you are now by acting as a mentor to you?
- If you're running your own company, what could you do to market yourself?

7 Finally, identify the actions you are prepared to take and when you're going to take them. Pinpoint any support you'll need and identify where you can get that from.

Focus on what you *can* change

Do something about the things you can change and don't waste time worrying about the things you cannot. When you look at the graduate recruitment market and your life after graduation, identify the things you can influence. If you're self employed, look at the way you organise your resources because you can influence the way you access and use them.

Pinpoint the missing angle which, once added, could lead to success

What do you need to do to turn your current position into a success and get to where you want to be? For example, you could consider:

1 Working for employers who naturally take on students with one or two years' experience after university. Why not find out how this route into the workplace would help you? Here your alumni associations with your old university could be invaluable.

2 Moving into an allied profession for a couple of years and then shifting track later, either in your own country or abroad.

3 Relocating now to where the opportunities are – which could be further afield than you like.

4 Working part time or on short-term stints until you find the right position. Go freelance!

5 Discussing your situation with relevant professional organisations; how flexible are the rules and regulations governing entry to and qualification for membership?

6   Starting your own business. There are lots of opportunities and programmes around for graduates who have business ideas, so find out what support and finance might be on offer and brainstorm that business idea!

7   Joining forces with fellow students from your course and brainstorming the issue together. What could you do collectively to turn the current situation into an opportunity?

Boost your creativity into solving problems and looking for opportunities. Get friends to help you brainstorm, and that way you're also tapping into their knowledge and creativity.

One option could be to work for one company for a couple of years and then to look to move into the company you'd really cherish a role with after that. Many employers take on graduates who have had a couple of years' experience elsewhere but find their talents aren't being fully appreciated or used.

What practical steps can you take?

There could be *practical* steps you need to take to blow barriers away. Let's look at some of them.

Get a coach

Career and business coaches help you identify what is important to you, what you want to achieve and what you need to do to make that happen. Some coaches work in a niche, for example, only with small creative companies and individuals to help them achieve their business and personal goals. Check that your coach is qualified and trained and find out what experience he or she has before parting with any money.

Identify your skills gaps

Look at anything which may boost your employability. For example, you could show your CV to a company and ask whether there is anything they think that's missing from your CV to get you into the work you want.

While waiting for a response ...

One of the traps writers tend to fall into is that they will send out a proposal to a publisher or editor and then wait for a response. What they should be doing is congratulating themselves for getting a proposal out; and then heading straight back to their desks to work on the next one. Don't fall into the same trap. As soon as you've finished work on one application, start on the next.

Don't be surprised or offended if you do not get a response to your application, speculative or otherwise. That's the real world. Get used to it! What can you do differently when you've qualified to help those who are coming through?

Be sure you understand the skills and toolkits employers are after

Companies will need particular skills and competencies sets such as applications and versions, but they may also have needs for people with softer skills, such as presenting to pitch for new business or dealing with the HR side of things if they are a small firm. If you have skills in a particular area or application, you could run an Internet search to look for companies using them which could in turn lead you to a potential future employer.

What specialist help is about to help you overcome any barriers you're hitting?

Many groups with special needs now have their own support networks, such as those who have had cancer or heart problems, mature workers, ex-offenders, those returning to the work after a break, people with disabilities, those with learning difficulties, asylum seekers, ethnic minorities, women – the list is simply endless. For example, if you have a disability, visit the website www.skill.org. uk to see how they can help you. Many professional bodies have a Young Professionals helpline or careers experts who can help you with advice and tips on any difficulties you are having.

How well are you selling yourself?

Think about the way you're selling yourself in terms of your approach, enthusiasm and passion for the industry. You need to show yourself as a person who can be trusted in the way you handle people and situations. Construct whole sentences, rather than using texting language that you'd send to your friends and family. Do not call people 'mate,' 'darling' or any other form of endearment. They are not your 'mates'.

Some simple do's and don'ts now follow. Patronising? No, they are merely included because of employers' comments regarding the lack of basic social skills and manners in many graduates. Practice a warm firm handshake with your friends, looking people in the eye. Keep your shoulders back and square and your head up. You can practice this with strangers you meet in everyday life. When you meet new people, use this handshake and smile. Drop the grunt; you're a graduate: sell yourself as such. Show yourself to be a positive, can do person. Leave the moods at home. We all get black days but there is no need to bring them to work. Do not whine about your current situation or blame past employers, teachers or anyone else for the state you are in. Be positive about going to university. You chose to do it and you gained from it, even though it may not seem like it right now.

Common concerns

I've just got a 2:2 ...
You're lucky. I've only got a third ...

Well, many employers are stipulating that yes, they do want a 2:1 or above and some are quite adamant that they won't consider anyone with lower than that. But there are plenty of good employers out there who *will* and your task now is to focus not on what you cannot change but what you can do and influence to get your foot in the door. Focus on what you *can* offer in the way of key skills, personal qualities and drive and motivation – things you can sell to an employer, who will want to know how you can contribute in the future. Could you work for that employer in a couple of years' time after getting some relevant experience behind you?

What about my age?

If you omit your age from your CV or application altogether, employers will wonder even more about your age. Use your date of birth (not your age e.g. 44 years) – it takes longer to work out so people are less likely to bother until later – and put it towards the end of your CV so that the recruiter can be excited about what you have to offer first. But, there are plenty of good things about being a mature worker and you should show that you mix easily with younger people (not mentioning children or grandchildren) in working situations, that you believe you can learn from each other, and get your image checked to make sure you look smart, crisp and fresh. Emphasise your work experience and the good points about maturity; many employers find mature staff more reliable. Show, too, that you can handle change well and that you're not stuck in your ways.

A company sponsoring me throughout my degree programme has suddenly said it can't take me on. Help!

First, think calmly. The probability is that market forces have caused such an event. Ask for feedback on your performance throughout the sponsorship. Then look at the positives – easier said than done if you were hoping that the sponsorship would lead straight into employment, but wallowing in sorrow won't change anything. You have probably acquired a lot of invaluable work experience as a result of your sponsorship, plus possibly financial benefits to boot. Put these to work for you now and make the experience you've had work for you. Your attitude alone can make or break your current situation, so don't dwell on what could have been – look forward.

Being successful abroad

The key to success with a move abroad is to immerse yourself totally into the culture and to meet as many locals as you can. If you stick with people of your own nationality, you might as well have stayed at home. Learn a little of the language before you go, at least enough to be able to say some pleasantries; if you can, talk to people who've worked there so that you know what to expect and what the differences will be. Take pictures of your family and friends to show new friends that you're human too. Enrol in a language school when you arrive to boost your skills. Read the local papers to find out what's happening and observe local customs and, in particular, dress. Ultimately, you want to win people over rather than alienate them. Watch, listen and observe and see what you can learn from people.

Learn from failure

If you're going to succeed in work, either as an entrepreneur or an employee, you need to be tough and tenacious, and to learn from failure. Two-thirds of all start ups fail in the first three years, for example, but many successful entrepreneurs point out that failure can be a tremendous learning tool. Failures give up their dreams and goals. They don't learn from the experience because they don't even try to see where they went wrong. They usually fall into the blame culture. Winners and successes may fail, but they learn from their failures and take the experience forward to build future successes.

Analyse failure, and you move forward. View it as part of the learning curve of life, and you'll come out much stronger for it. The tough times in life show you that you have what it takes to survive and come out of situations on top. As you get older, you realise how much you've grown from all those difficult times in work and personal lives. We all hit rough patches in life, like an aircraft going through turbulence, but we usually come out of it all the stronger for it. When you look back on something in this context, if you learn from an experience, you can hardly describe it as failure.

Don't take failure personally

If you didn't get that much cherished job you wanted, perhaps it simply wasn't meant to be – maybe someone else was simply a better fit for the post and the company. Take your 'failure' with you in the next interview and you won't win any friends. Invest in a punch bag or have a workout at the gym instead, obtain feedback if you can and review your performance yourself.

Ten survival steps to coping with failure

1   Have faith in yourself – there will be that perfect position for you somewhere out there, but you need to know what you're looking for. Keep focused and keep trying.
2   Keep knocking at doors. Get help and support around you, both experts in the field and your friends and family.
3   Ask for advice on turning those potential applications into sure bets.
4   Look for new strategies.
5   Keep a sense of perspective.

6 Don't turn to comfort eating, drink or drugs. It won't change anything. Keep healthy.

7 Learn from those who have failed but picked themselves up and gone on to be successful.

8 Obstacles in our way are often our unwillingness to say 'no' to people, or our belief in ourselves as much as anything real or physical.

9 Push yourself out of your boundary zone at every opportunity you get. You'll be surprised how much you can achieve.

10 Live life differently if you can. A fresh approach works wonders and avoids your getting stuck in a rut.

Self-employed and ...

Someone's pinched my idea!

If you're going to create and implement designs or ideas or anything of that ilk, you'll want copyrights, patents and trademarks. Protect your own ideas and designs by making full use of the support available to you, such as:

- ACID – Anti Copying in Design www.acid.uk.com
- Institute of Trade Mark Attorneys www.itma.org.uk
- Usability Professionals' Association www.upassoc.org
- Own It www.own-it.org

Finally, the Charter on Intellectual Property promoted a new user-friendly way of handing out intellectual property rights in 2005, written by an international group of artists, scientists, lawyers, politicians, academics and business experts.

Needing help on a particular aspect of your journey?

Look to meet with colleagues and other like-minded professionals, to share best practice and benefit from each other's experience, expertise and network. Many of these will have individuals you can tap into for expert help and advice. These vary in the way in which they are organised and in the help they can give you. BusinessLink's network can help you, firstly, to set up your own business, and secondly, to grow the business, with help and information in areas such as exploiting your ideas, employing people, health and safety, premises, international trade, finance, grants and guidance on the rules and regulations applying to businesses in the sector you wish to work in.

Not getting the contracts?

If you're in a line of work in which contracting is all the rage, and you're having difficulty picking them up, think about what is working for you and what is not. Contact people who have decided not to buy or pursue your product or service, and ask for some feedback. Is there anything in your sales pitch which did not endear them to your sale? What could you have done differently to achieve a different outcome? If there was nothing, were you looking in the right place for clients to start with, or pricing it properly? Obtain business advice, either from local business advisers or specific industry bodies.

Summary action points

Identify barriers and obstacles and then do something about them through creative thinking.

1 Identify what barriers and obstacles you have ahead of you which may hinder you achieving your goals.
2 Now pinpoint as many ways to tackle them as you can.
3 Identify the one which will work best for you and do it.

Chapter 9

Moving on ... Your future

No matter who you work for, careers and businesses need nurturing and loving care just like any relationship in life. Look after them, devote time, energy, thought and planning to them, and focus on them, they will blossom. Allow them to bumble along, and they will degenerate into just a job.

First, though, you need to walk before you can run

So you've signed your contract of employment and you know you're expected to hit the ground running. What can you do to help yourself? Some ideas are:

1 Could you spend a couple of hours in the office meeting colleagues *before* your official start date, a bit like a "freshers' week at work" condensed into a few hours?

2 Check the dress code. Work out what you're going to wear each day in that first week. Make sure it's clean and pressed.

3 Prepare meals in advance and buy what you need. Familiarise yourself with the area you'll work in, so that you know where the nearest chemist/sandwich shop, etc. is.

4 Check that you have the documents you need for your first day, such as a P45.

Once you've started, however nervous you are, keep smiling. Most people remember their first day; they will want to put you at ease, but don't burn yourself out by being overly friendly in the first few hours. Ask for a buddy who can help and guide you if you have questions about the place, someone you can turn to for advice and information. Talk to people by the coffee machine and join them for lunch. They are human, after all. Offer a friendly firm handshake as you meet people.

Find out about the company policy regarding mobiles and personal emails; and before you put any information online, such as blogs, consider how it could be used. Keep your own counsel; don't shoot your mouth off. Pick your confidantes and true work friends with care. Confidential means just that.

It may take several weeks and months to hit the ground running

Starting work in any company can be frustrating for a few weeks. You want to prove yourself and settle in. Yet being in a new work environment is just like being in a country you've never visited before, with lots to learn: how the computer system works, and whether there is an intranet; whose approval you need for what; who the key decision makers are; what the arrangements are vis-à-vis coffee and tea breaks/where you get them/whether you pay for them; and what people do at lunch time. You'll also learn who is who, what is where, and try to remember names and what people do. At the same time you want to make an impact, so:

1   Be friendly, but don't call people 'mate'. They are not your mates (yet); they are work colleagues;
2   Listen and learn how things work before you dive in with comments; find out the history behind something which looks strange to you before you make suggestions;
3   Ask people questions about themselves and their role to make friends at work and learn who does what;
4   Prove you're a safe pair of hands to be trusted and a team player who fits in; be willing to stay late to get things done and double-check your work for accuracy;
5   Be ready to begin at the bottom and use the opportunity to learn as much as you can about the way the organisation functions.

And then, of course, there's life outside the working hours you're now doing

There's the added stress of handling full-time work five days a week at a time the employer dictates, and doing all those small but essential tasks needed to keep life ticking along smoothly. If you spend eight hours a day sleeping (56 hours a week) and nine hours a day working, including the commute to work, that leaves you with 67 hours a week to do your admin, banking and pay bills; laundry and ironing, cleaning and shopping, cooking, eating and washing up, personal hygiene and, more occasionally, check ups with the doctor, dentist, hygienist, and taking the car to the garage for an MOT. You may keenly miss the freedom of your student days when you could pretty much decide what to do when, especially when you take into account that you'll probably also want time to socialise, catch up with old mates, remembering your parents, enjoy leisure hobbies, exercise, having weekends away and that all important 'me' down time to re-charge your batteries. Build strong supportive career and life networks around you, as Chapter 4 outlined.

On top of all that, you may have enrolled to study for professional qualifications and further learning.

Qualifying as a professional

At any stage of your career, talk to your current employer to ask about support for your on-going professional development, such as study leave or financial help, perhaps paying for all or part of the course, or your study materials or examinations. When approaching the subject, show how the studies will boost your effectiveness on the job and benefit your employer, so that you present a 'win–win' situation.

Every professional organisation has specific guidelines laid down to ensure that its members attain a particular standard and status. These standards will be clearly laid out online and in printed literature. Some have mentors who can help you with your time management and learning organisation, both essential ingredients to success. Talk through what you need to do to qualify with your own employer and work out an action plan to ensure you get exposure to the right experience and skills, courses and study.

Enlist the help of:

1   Young professionals who have been where you are; be inspired and motivated by what their professional status has done for them and the strategies they used to ensure their success.
2   The careers advisers in professional organisations who will have seen people in most predicaments before. Get to know one.
3   Your employer's experience. Could they give you a buddy to help you through?
4   Your line manager; engage him or her in your progression and success and be clear about what help you need and projects you need to undertake to gain the right experience.
5   Your peers. Motivate and help each other.
6   Yourself. Focus your time and energy on what is important.

Work out the time which is best for you to study – you know when you work best and at your most effective. It requires real motivation and dedication to hit the books at 5 a.m. while the rest of the world sleeps, or switch onto your studies while your mates are cheering your favourite football team on in the pub. Remind yourself of the benefits of professional status and qualifying; keep them at the forefront of your mind. The benefits you'll accrue as a result of your new found status will keep you going when times get tough.

On-going CPD

It will probably be essential for you to continue with your learning and training after you've achieved professional status on an annual basis to update you on new technologies, skills, developments and knowledge. Discuss your needs with your employer or contact the most relevant professional body to assess what you need to do to meet this commitment. Plan your CPD well ahead in the year to ensure that you meet any necessary targets and can select something which will truly enhance your effectiveness and which really interests you. As well as boosting your technical skills and expertise related to the work you do, however, remember to consider both your business and soft skills, too, such as leadership and managing others. An MBA may be just the ticket.

What about an MBA?

Many engineers work as technical specialists and then want to move on into project management or further, and an MBA gives them the management knowledge and tools to do just that. It helps boost business acumen, a lack of which could prevent you from taking a more commercial role. Consider how far you want to go. Do you want to become a leader in the FTSE or NASDAQ 100 companies, creating a vision for your company and leading others to implement it for you? Would you like to set up your own business once you have experience and qualifications behind you? What skills and qualifications do you need to get there?

If you're considering doing an MBA, contact the Association of MBAs which represents the international MBA community: its students, graduates, schools, businesses and employers. The Association promotes the MBA as a leading management qualification and aims to encourage management education at post-graduate level to create highly competent professional managers. There are MBA fairs in the UK during the year and the Association can provide you with more information on those.

Keeping up-to-date

Sign up for your professional organisation's newsletters and magazines, university and research institutes' newsletters, so that you can really keep up-to-date with developments. Network, so that you can recommend experts in different parts of the industry and talk knowledgeably enough about it so as to portray yourself as someone who can signpost others in the right direction. Keep an eye on international sources of information, such as the EDN site, with its various pages relevant to regions and countries in the world such as Asia, China, Japan, Europe and Australia. Can you contribute to their pages and news, views and discussion forums and help shape the direction your field takes?

Boost your language skills!

Employers are well aware of the benefits of having a workforce who can talk to customers and clients in their own language. Many companies are seeing the benefits first hand of having employees who can speak their customers' languages, through increased sales, improved business and personal relationships and a clearer understanding of what is required. Boost your language capabilities if you truly want to have a later career in management. Show you can embrace other cultures and kick off meetings by trying to speak your client's language. People always appreciate the effort.

Developing yourself and others

Governments worldwide are seeking to boost their citizens' skills and capabilities in the battle to be competitive. In the UK for example, Sector Skills Councils (www.ssda.org.uk) are working to ensure that employers have the skills they need in the future. National Skills Academies for the Construction sector have been established with this end in mind, particularly to support the construction of the Olympic facilities in London.

New Sector Skills Councils include:

- SEMTA (science, engineering, manufacturing and technology industries) at www.semta.org.uk
- Proskills (the process and manufacturing centre) at www.proskills.co.uk
- Lantra (the environmental and land based industries) at www.lantra.co.uk
- Go Skills at www.goskills.org for the passenger transport sector
- Skillset at www.skillset.org/games/ for the audio-visual industries
- Skills for logistics at www.skillsforlogistics.org/
- SummitSkills (building services engineering) at www.summitskills.org.uk/
- Construction Skills at www.constructionskills.net – working in partnership with the CITB (Construction Skills), the Construction Industry Council (www.cic.org.uk) and the CITB Northern Ireland (www.citbni.org.uk).

Visit their sites to find out how they could help you and your career, and you and your business. Why not see if you can contribute towards their efforts?

Get devoted to lifelong learning

View training as an investment which boosts your employability. As a graduate, you're more likely to ask for training because you are used to identifying your own training and learning needs and making sure they are met. Your university studies will have taught you how to learn through many methods, which will prepare you well for training and learning at work. Identify where your skills gaps are and what you need to do to close that gap.

So what happens next?

There are a number of 'what' and 'where' and 'how' questions here. What have you achieved so far? Where do you see your career going next? Which potential barriers or obstacles may hinder your progress? Which extra skills will give you more openings in the employment market? If you are working for an industry which thrives on employing contractors, you will need to be particularly proactive in networking and promoting yourself. Some sites have advice for people who have been made redundant or pages to offer support to contractors and project managers or forums via which you can contact your peers for help, contacts and advice.

A dogged, persistent effort is essential to take you to career success, in which these skills will be essential:

* Self-awareness
  Knowing your strengths, weaknesses, passions, ambitions, values and needs
* Self-promotion
  Raising your profile in the organisation and sector
* Exploring and creating opportunities
  Being proactive in taking responsibility for your own career development
* Decision making and action planning
  Making informed, decisive decisions that will take you in the right direction and working out what needs to be done and when
* Coping with uncertainty
  Dealing with redundancy, restructuring, new clients, new tomorrows
* Transfer of skills
  Thinking laterally and broadly, applying the commonalities to the workplace and life

- Self-belief and confidence
  Yes, you can do it!
- Willingness to learn
  New products, new technology, new skills
- Commitment/dependability
  Everyone knowing you're a safe pair of hands, and management and your own staff trusting you
- Self-motivation
  Having drive and enthusiasm, and taking the initiative
- Co-operation
  People wanting to have you on board their team
- Knowledgeable about new developments in the field
  Showing that you're up-to-date.

Plot and plan your next steps effectively, pinpointing the learning and experiences you will need to get to the next stage. Set yourself a long-term goal and break it down into manageable steps. Keep these at the forefront of your mind. This applies whether you are looking to climb the career or housing ladder, build a new circle of friends or work on a project for your company. While everyone else sleeps and parties, work at your goal. You'll soon climb the career ladder through your own dogged determination, persistence and perseverance while they are left dozing or snoring their way through the working week.

Getting promoted

If you want to move up, plan for it and prepare a path. For instance, if you get the chance to train any new staff or take responsibility for a group, do it; such an action will give your employer a chance to see how you put your management skills into action. Show how effective you are and tell your boss about the results you're getting. Watch the behaviours of those higher up and ask them what has worked for them. Visit your professional organisation's website for advice. The Institution of Engineering and Technology, for example, has tips, information and advice on career and professional development, mentoring, job hunting and changing career.

Review your progress regularly

Make sure you have a regular review, so that you can improve your performance and assess your progress. Are you on track to achieve your career goals in the timescale you want? How can you handle your workload more effectively and time efficiently while maintaining or improving your performance? Are you clear about what your role is and how that contributes to the organisation's vision? Does your team understand it too? As you progress, put a managerial hat on, rather than a technical one, and take a higher helicopter view looking at the bigger picture. Delegate where you can, developing those you supervise through coaching, mentoring and one-to-one training. Assess whether you need any extra skills or qualifications to progress your path, such as an MBA or a post-graduate or professional studies.

A strong network right across a company could smooth your path into new roles and it will raise your profile. Get on a committee so that other people can see how you perform. Dress for the role you aspire to, not the role you're in.

Watch office politics!

To safeguard yourself as high as you can against redundancy:

1   Maintain a high profile;
2   Become indispensable; be the company expert on something, the one everyone turns to;
3   Watch the bottom line and continually suggest ways of cutting it without affecting the service offered to the customer or client;
4   Be creative by designing new systems and approaches and taking everyone on board at the same time;
5   Join a cross-company committee or project which raises your profile and gets you noticed by other people;
6   Bring in new clients and customers.

Get a strong network across the company – people you can call on for help, advice, information or support when the occasion demands it and who you can equally say 'let's grab a beer or a coffee' when it doesn't. Keep up-to-date with each other's sections and what they are doing. Be discerning, however. Watch what you share, so that you don't break any confidentiality rules, or jeopardise your own position by talking about your own career plans. Confide in those you truly trust.

Know your worth

Prior to your reviews, find out what the industry pays someone with your experience and qualifications, but don't forget that perks can make a huge difference to the overall package. Many agencies have salary reviews on their websites. Collect evidence of your contribution to the company, plus your research on pay and put your case forward for a rise if you want one. Don't expect to get an immediate answer. Be prepared to negotiate: there are ways and means to enhance your overall package.

Leaving your current employer

It's not working out!

If you think things aren't going well as you try to settle into a new job, give it time. Ask for feedback on your performance and try to identify what it is that is not quite right. For example, do you feel you're being held back, and that your career and salary potential are being limited by your current company, or that you need more support from your boss or line-manager? If you decide that you need to move on, having given this first post its all, view this first role as a stepping stone to something better. Many employers appreciate that it can take a couple of attempts to get the match of employer and role right, and some even deliberately take on graduates with a couple of years' experience after their degree, with the understanding that the first role might not have lived up to their expectations or worked out. Whatever you do, do *not* bad-mouth your current employer in future interviews. It will do you no good. Be positive about what you've learnt and contributed to your current role and how you've progressed, but also be clear about your ambitions and aspirations.

Time to move on

If you think you're coming to a dead-end in your current role, take stock of where you are. Before you hand in your notice, ensure that there are absolutely no other opportunities at your current company. Consider what you have done to create opportunities for expanding your role and taking on new projects and responsibilities. What is right with the job you have now? Often there's plenty we like about our work, and it's the bits we don't like that we tend to focus on and gripe about.

Now look forward. Have your ambitions got lost in the current role you're in? Before you decide whether you can achieve them with your current employer, talk to your boss and/or human resources and put an action plan together to help you get back on track. If your current employer cannot meet your future aspirations, *then* research a move to another organisation or set up business on your own. Get the new deal signed before giving in your notice. Be discreet, and don't work at your CV in work time on a work PC. Use the Internet and specialist agencies, your network and company websites to help you find that next right move.

Remaining connected

These sites may help:

- www.engineeringalley.com – a worldwide engineering directory and resource with details of agencies, training programmes and more
- www.engineering.co.uk/ – trade leads, events, exhibitions, vacancies, forums, links
- www.engcen.com/index.asp – Engineering Central, mostly US-based, with jobs and help on resume writing at entry level and beyond, plus a salary wizard.

Redundancy

If you were suddenly made redundant, and or there was a downswing in the market, without any notice whatsoever, one of the key things you need to get you back on your feet and out there job hunting fast is a strong network. This means covering basis such as:

1   Professional organisations; what help they can give people such as yourself who have been made redundant;
2   Upholding the ethics of the industry – being someone whom others can refer on to people without hesitation;

3   Considering whether you'd move locations if the right job was situated at the other end of the country or the other side of the world;
4   Maintaining links with relevant recruitment consultants and online agencies;
5   Updating your CV regularly;
6   Keeping in touch with people in your network;
7   Responding to requests for help from people who need your help – one day you could be on the phone asking for help from them;
8   Showing a willingness to learn and move into new roles when you're talking to your line-manager or boss;
9   A recognition that redundancy is not the end of the world and can in fact be the start of something new, exciting and terrific;
10   Savings in the bank for as many months' salary as you can gather – it gives you time to think;
11   A sure knowledge of the sector you work in and a passion for it which you exude to everyone you speak to;
12   An understanding of what (local) government networks are available and how they can help;
13   Creating your own luck;
14   Using relevant trade publications and sites to secure that next role.

Going abroad

How competent are you to handle overseas assignments and an international career?

Finding work

Use all your networks to ask about new projects and developments which need skilled workers. *The Asian Report* outlines new projects in the development, planning, engineering, procurement and construction phases and it gives companies which are looking for new people with the right expertise the facility to advertise their needs online. It covers areas such as Indonesia, Asia, Australia, China, India and Russia, to name a few. It details the positions available, their location, the experience, qualifications and skills needed, a brief description of the project and contact details, should you wish to follow up the opportunity.

The website www.expatnetwork.com/ is a very useful site for expatriates working abroad, including a salary survey, international jobs, lifestyle and money, health and more. There's even an Expats for Kids link!

Heading to other shores – working abroad

This may be appropriate if you're thinking, *'Well, my industry is dead in this country. So what now?'* In this case, you have a couple of choices before you. You can switch to an allied industry, in which your degree may still come in useful; or you can change altogether, or start your own business. Could you for example export anything which is needed by the industry in those regions where it is flourishing? This could be easier than you think, thanks to the Internet. Find out more from the Institute of Export. And of course, you could consider these questions: *'Where else is it functioning?'*, *'How might it use my skills?'*, *'Should I head out there for a holiday and see what's happening and whether there might be anything for me in that region?'* If you choose to stay put, hard though this sounds, there is no point in whining about it because such an action won't change anything (which is why it will be all the more frustrating). Consider alternatives.

Ten questions to ask include:

1   What is the local job market like?
2   How do employers recruit staff there? What is involved?
3   How should I write a CV for that country?
4   Which organisations and websites can I turn to for advice and information, such as Prospects and Hobsons?
5   Does my professional body or trade organisation have any relevant links in the country I wish to work in? What support can it give me?
6   How will my current qualifications transfer? Will they be accepted? Are these countries more interested in experience than academic qualifications or vice versa?
7   How does the working environment differ? What is acceptable behaviour and what is not?

8   What level of job would I have with the competences I have? Will I need to take additional tests to prove my competence in my new country before I can start work?

9   Where in the world will my knowledge and skills be needed in the future?

10   What sort of situations are you prepared to get yourself into?

The last question relates to the element of risk you're prepared to take overseas. Whilst employers (may) take every effort to guarantee your safety, risk can never really be eroded. Six months in a high risk area may bring you lots of money and adventure, but how will it affect family and friends safely back home?

If you're asked to take such a contract:

1   Obtain advice from your consulate as to the current situation in the country;

2   Learn more than a few words of the local language. It may help break the ice or give you a head start in conversations where it is assumed that you don't speak a word;

3   Ensure your affairs are in order back home, including making a will;

4   Find out from talking to other employees or contract workers in the region what life is like there before you head out or sign on the dotted line.

Put 'Willing to relocate' on your CV or business card but be prepared to actually do it. If you're focusing in on one country and you satisfy visa requirements, say so on your CV or covering letter (see www.workpermit.com). Look out for events and newspaper supplements promoting life or companies abroad. Use your network to help you get work overseas. Read journals and newspapers. Use embassies and State employment services such as www.europa.eu.int/eures. The European Job Mobility Portal is one of the places where European candidates can see an employer's vacancy and employers can multi-search for CVs which may meet their needs. It links the public employment services in Europe and helps people take up work in other member states of the EEA. It has lots of information on jobs, learning, labour markets, health, registering for work when you arrive, and working conditions.

You could also sign up with a recruitment agency with international offices or connections, or go through an organisation offering placements abroad, such as GAP, or just get on with it yourself. Twinning arrangements and Chamber of Commerce organisations (www.chamberonline.co.uk/) may also be helpful. Their site has details of all the UK Chambers, overseas Chambers in the UK, British Chambers of Commerce overseas and Council of British Chambers of Commerce in Continental Europe. It also has an excellent export zone and business services on offer.

How well do your qualifications travel?

Professional organisations are increasingly working together to enable their members to work abroad with greater ease while ensuring a high standard of qualification and competence cross-borders. Those relating to engineering and the built environment are well ahead of the game. Visit the International Engineering Agreements website at www.ieagreements.com/ for example, and you'll find details of six such arrangements which will facilitate your move abroad. The Engineers' Mobility Forum (www..iagreements.com/EMF/default.cfm) and the APEC Engineer Agreement form facilitate (global) movement, APEC standing for Asia-Pacific Engineering Co-operation. Your professional body may have experience in helping members work overseas and they may also be able to link you up to networking groups in the area from which you can meet like-minded people and make friends even before leaving home.

If you are an EU resident wishing to work elsewhere in the EU, visit the Department for Education and Skills' site at www.dfes.gov.uk/europeopen/ which tells you how to prove your competence to work in another EU, EEA or Swiss country. And for details on comparability of qualifications between the EU and UK, you should visit www.naric.ac.uk, website for the National Recognition Information Centre for the United Kingdom.

If you're taking your UK qualification with you to work abroad, you can contact services offered by NARIC's colleagues via NARIC's site. They cover a huge list of countries such as Azerbaijan, Belarus and Armenia.

Heading to the danger zone

You may be willing to help out or looking for experience in more dangerous waters, in which case www.dangerzonejobs.com is for you. Not for the fainthearted, either the person who is re-locating to do the job or their families back home.

Volunteer Service Overseas place people for up to two years to work in countries needing help. Find out more at www.vso.org.uk Finally, where there are catastrophes in the world, there will be a need for engineers, construction workers and disaster management specialists to rebuild communities and the infrastructure required to make them habitable again. Visit professional organisations' sites to find out more about the opportunities to get out there and help or those of the Foreign Office, and www.redr.org, which has offices in Australia, Canada, India, Kenya, New Zealand and the UK and members elsewhere too.

Getting advice on the dangers

The Foreign Office at www.fco.gov.uk has country profiles and updates and news on travel, with travel advice for specific countries, general travel information (visas, health (including bird flu), insurance, terrorism) and travel checklists. The UK Department of Health (www.dh.gov.uk/PolicyAndGuidance/fs/en) has excellent advice for travellers.

Heading off into the blue is all very well and international experience looks fantastic on your CV, but consider your loved ones and a return home

If you are thinking of re-locating, talk through the idea with your dependants if you have any. Be sure that they will be happy to either have you suddenly relocated to a remote corner of China or Afghanistan at a week's notice while they stay put; or that they are content to uproot and join you there. Some companies may simply be transferring you abroad, rather than your offspring and partners who may not form part of the package. Others may enable your loved ones to go with you, but there may be visa and/or lifestyle restrictions limiting the lives you live or your partner's ability to work. Equally, depending on the age of your children, such a move could affect their status as they plan their university education – they may be viewed as overseas students. Consider, also, how your salary and career may be affected by a move abroad – enlist the views of other professionals via online forums and your own network. When you're looking at any financial provision for your future, check to see what the taxation implications are if you move about. How will working abroad affect any pension due to you later in life, for example? A good accountant with international experience should be able to help you. Read *Working Abroad, The Complete Guide to Overseas Employment* by Jonathan Reuvid (see Further Reading at the end of this book).

That's life!

Handling misconceptions of the role

It may be a huge source of annoyance to you that people find it hard to understand what goes on in your world, just as they may find it equally frustrating that you do not comprehend theirs. The world of engineering and the built environment can be specially misunderstood in view of the way the term 'engineer' is being applied now, for example to 'domestic engineer'. Use easy examples of the impact your work has and how you are involved in the process. If your patience runs out, point people in the direction of the website www. discoverengineering.org which explains it all very simply.

Giving something back

Do you want to give something back, and if so, how? For example, would you like to:

◆ Help shape the future careers of young professionals coming through by offering advice, being a mentor and coach to them?
◆ Get involved in the international community, contributing to the network?
◆ Raise the profile of engineering (or any other career you have) either to young people making career choices or in society as a whole? For example, could you help out at careers events and give talks in schools?
◆ Use your skills voluntarily, perhaps helping where there has been a disaster or where completion of a particular project will make a huge difference to peoples' lives?

Working with universities

What benefits can you enjoy from engaging with your old university? You could:

1   Help graduates coming through the system, perhaps by contributing towards the delivery of careers support to those in your subject areas;
2   Ask university staff to deliver continued professional development sessions at any local events you're holding;
3   Benefit from the research and development being undertaken by the universities themselves. How can *your* company benefit from the excellent research efforts being undertaken there? What local initiatives are available to encourage the transfer of knowledge to local universities? The website www.hero. ac.uk will tell you more (see Useful Addresses at the end of this book);
4   Join forces with the relevant department at your university by working on a project or innovation together;
5   Give students a real live work project to get stuck into which you need doing but don't have the internal resources to do;
6   Use your university's products and services such as undertaking product testing and clinical trials, the use of consultancy services, lab facilities, access to research undertaken by them, the use of science parts and innovation services.

Make the most of your professional body

Many professional bodies have different types of membership depending on the stage you are at in your career. Are you progressing your level of membership to match your experience? There may be categories for students, graduates, young professionals, fully fledged professionals and sometimes, fellows, reserved for the most senior, experienced, qualified members of the body.

Changing career

Many people take up post-graduate study as a way to change direction but you don't have to go to such lengths in many sectors. Ensure that you really are ready for a change and not simply fed up with the job you're in at the moment or in need of new responsibilities. Only proceed when you're absolutely sure that there is nothing left for you in the world and company you're with now. Changing career is not easily undertaken so you need to be sure you're doing the right thing. Consider what you want in your new career and how you want it to be different from your current one. Identify the skills you want to use, the sector you want to work in and the impact you want to make. Once you have a clear idea of where you're going, you can set out to make it happen. Look for guidance and advice for those who are already doing what you want to do. People love to talk about themselves and you will find that they are more than happy to talk to you.

Be ready to adapt to succeed. You could take a sideways move with an organisation you're with to get into a role you really crave, or start afresh in another company at a lower level to achieve that change of career you really wanted, or set up your own business or buy a franchise.

So you've set up your own business and want to go for growth?

Consider these questions:

- What have you achieved to date?
- What are your strengths, weaknesses, opportunities and threats?
- Where do you see your business going in the next year? The next five years?
- What extra resources do you need, e.g. time, money, equipment?
- Who can help you with that?
- What new products or services are you creating/innovating?
- What extra staff if any do you need and how will you find and employ them?
- What are you doing to build your niche and brand?
- What are your financial targets for the year?
- How much time are you devoting to business planning?
- What can you outsource, leaving yourself to focus on developing the business?
- What are you doing to get feedback from your customers to enhance the prospect of repeat business?

- Which marketing methods are proving to be most effective?
- What three new ways can you think of to market your business?
- What three new things can you think of to surprise and delight existing customers?
- Which comes first: business or lifestyle?

Looking to leave the day job behind

You may be working in the day to get some money coming in and tackling your 'real' job at night, hoping to resign when you hit a breakthrough. If this sounds like you, make sure your 'night' job is honestly going places by asking the following questions:

- What have you achieved overall so far?
- What is working well?
- Where can you create more time in your day?
- Where do you want to be in six months' time?
- What will you need to do to make that happen?
- Who can help you further?
- What do you need to do to move your business to the next stage?
- How can you add value to your products and services so as to bring in extra income and enable you to focus more on the business and reduce the time you're spending on the day job?

Flexibility and adaptability go a long way to making the most of life

You may be merrily making your way through your career and then something happens which changes everything for you at a stroke.

Ten events which could change your life and your career

1   You meet your future partner; and life is never the same;
2   You create a baby and parenthood is on the way;
3   You hit on a business or social idea which, if implemented, will really make a difference;

4   You or one or your relatives or a friend falls seriously ill or has an accident and needs special care and love; plus it makes you re-think;
5   You get headhunted;
6   A major world event makes you rethink life;
7   You volunteer for a cause you believe in;
8   You decide to live abroad;
9   You win the lottery;
10   You take the decision that you want to live a higher quality life and set about doing just that.

Summary action points

Take responsibility for enhancing your own employability:

1   Keep a track of any ways in which recruitment methods for your sector change.
2   Who are the key players in the market you're in for recruitment? Who are the main agencies?
3   Don't stay with an employer if they're not enabling you to meet your career goals. Move on.

Chapter 10

Here's to life!

Take a holistic view of your life, and good health and happiness are more likely to be yours. Take a narrow, focused view of it, concentrating on only one aspect, and the others areas will suffer. There will be times when one aspect of your life – such as your career – takes priority over others. But that doesn't mean that the rest of your life should lose out totally. If you're not fit and healthy for example, it will be harder to maintain a peak performance at work and enjoy life – which could make all the difference to whether you get that promotion or make that next step or not. Continually look at your life to consider questions such as:

- What do you want in your life besides your career?
- Who do you want in your life?
- What are you doing to enjoy life?
- What are you doing to pay off your loans?
- What are you doing to start building financial security for yourself?

We just have one life, so make time for those things which matter to you most, such as family, friends and fun. The way you manage your resources – time, energy, money, health and relationships – can make a huge difference to the quality of life you enjoy.

What are the things you want in your life to be happy and fulfilled? Do any of the examples in Table 10.1 below feature?

From the day we are born, life often gets in the way, throwing trials, tribulations and challenges at us. Working towards some 'wants' and 'must haves' in your life may demand that you 'park' other things aside for several weeks or months while you focus on them or a project that is of particular importance to you – such as your wedding day or training for a marathon. But a balance helps keep things

Table 10.1

Family – perhaps children	Key relationships and roles
Pets	Fun and laughter
Friends	Volunteering
Travel	Cultural and leisure activities
Dreams	Nature
Adventure	Excitement
Material goods	A good sex life
Achievements	Nice place to live
Financial assets	Solid retirement plans
Health and vitality	Great memories
Spirituality	Other

in perspective. And the work–life balance becomes a hot topic as individuals struggle to find ways to cope with the demands of work and personal commitments to family and friends. Balance is important in many aspects of life and Table 10.2 below gives suggestions as to where this balance is important.

How balanced is *your* life?

Every year, check your work–life balance is as you want. Assess how content you are with each area of your life which is important to you and to pinpoint those which need work and which you want to change.

Try this exercise to assess how well balanced your life is. For each of the categories you ticked in Table 10.1, consider:

1   How satisfied are you right now with each one? Rate them individually from 0 to 10. Totally satisfied earns a 10; complete dissatisfaction a 0.
2   How does your life look? How many segments are a 10?

Table 10.2

Work	and	Leisure
Work	and	Holidays
Rest	and	Exercise
Healthy food	and	A bit of what you fancy
Smooth running of life	and	Challenges
Certainty	and	Uncertainty

3   Which ones need working on (i.e. are below a 7)? What would they have to be like for you to rank them as a 10?
4   What do you need to do to make that happen?
5   What will you do to make them happen and when?
6   You can keep doing this exercise over and over, enabling you to make the changes you want in your life through a continual process of making sure that every one is a 10, or at least working towards it. In addition, you can repeat the exercise breaking down one element into various segments or units and grading each of them out of 10. Health and fitness might be divided into areas such as fitness, healthy eating, chill time, stretching and flexibility and smoking.

But work's taken over my life!

More employees are now finding that short breaks recharge their batteries quite adequately without a huge panic about sorting out the in-tray before and after a longer break. A good proportion put off their holidays and don't take the full allowance *'I'm too busy at work'*. Very few of us can keep going at premium performance without having some sort of regular break built into the day. Our own bodies have their own needs; one person may be able to do with very little sleep, while others need a lot. If you don't listen to your body, sooner or later it will pay you back when you least need it, to remind you that it has needs too, such as *proper* rest and recuperation. You're not indispensable. It's sad to say, but if you were killed by a bus today, your company *would* go on without you. If you don't look after yourself, you are unlikely to be able to take care of others.

There are some careers in which long hours are the norm, but it can be easy to fall into the trap of doing long hours for the sake of it. The person who never takes a lunch break can rarely work at the same performance level throughout the day. The person who always takes a break away from the phone, email and work environment can only find her performance enhanced. No excuses! Walk around the block for 20 minutes and boost your heart beat, reduce your stress levels, keep that weight down *and* boost your mood.

Stress

With all the hype about stress, remember that the right sort of stress can help you live longer. Mild to moderate stress increases the production of brain cells, enabling them to function at peak capacity, so if you want to live life to a peak performance, get stressed but in the right way – it makes your body and mind stronger.

Beneficial stress gives you recovery time and a sense of accomplishment afterwards. It challenges you, although you may complain about it at the time. The bad stuff is prolonged, repeated, sustained and unrewarding. You need to find the middle ground between the two and build it into your daily life. Look for activities which reward and stimulate you, such as a run before work, studying in the evenings or voluntary work at weekends.

Get out of your comfort zone and take part in something which isn't routine and predictable or effortless. The more you look for these sorts of activities, the more you'll benefit. Collapsing in front of the TV after a day's work with a glass of wine isn't beneficial. Playing some sort of sport or going to adult education is. It's important to face stress or challenges mentally, physically, socially and spiritually. Give yourself proper 'chill' time. Don't waste time dwelling on the problems and demands of life – think about the pleasure, variety and vigour that challenges bring us and you'll feel much more alert and in control. Many challenges arrive through the roles we choose to play in life.

What roles do you want to play?

We all have roles in life and they all tend to appear at different times. Table 10.3 below shows roles most of us experience in our lives.

Our roles and relationships and the responsibilities that come with them intertwine with careers more than any other aspect of life. Which comes first: career or ageing relative? The presentation or a sick child? The school play or your squash game? The carer in us may play a key role and take centre stage in our lives while our parents get older and need decisions to be made for them. The parent has a lifelong role, but spends more time on it in the early years of a child's life and that role changes as life progresses, such that their children become their friends in adulthood. Our relationships with our siblings change, too, particularly as we all settle down into adult life and face the challenges of dealing with ageing parents.

Table 10.3

Parent	Friend
Son/daughter	Volunteer
Manager	Leader
Supervisor	Confidante
Doer	Thinker
Teacher	Adviser
Loner	Niece/nephew
Aunt/uncle	Grandparent
Actor	Diplomat
Neighbour	Carer
Sister/brother	Cousin
Good Samaritan	Hero

Our friends, too, change. We keep some throughout life; others we see enter at different stages and then leave, as if they came for a reason. Perhaps they were there to teach us something, to make us laugh at a time when we felt low, to make us feel good about ourselves, or just ... because. We need friends, both on our own account and when with a partner. Friends help you to keep things in perspective. A true friend is there for the good and bad times and will see you through.

If we're to have successful, empowering relationships, we need to put boundaries on what we will and won't do in our role. We may tire of the friend who calls us just once too often in the early hours of the morning, distraught over a break-up. We may be fed up of being the only sibling who makes an effort with our parents, while our siblings bleat that they are 'too busy'. Assertiveness is important if friendships and relationships are to thrive and grow. Saying 'no' is important in any role, if we are to feel strong and right. Saying 'yes' to keep the peace usually leads to feelings of resentment and disappointment in ourselves for not having the courage to say what we really want to say. Saying 'no' is a sign that we feel confident enough in ourselves to say what we mean and, crucially, that we care about ourselves and what we undertake in life.

The ability to manage yourself and others impacts on your ability to be personally effective in work and life. For example, if you have children, you will need to motivate them and get the family working as a team on projects to create a cohesive family unit. There will be times when you need to manage your own temper, when they do something which drives you to distraction for the hundredth time. Similarly, you will need to manage your client relationships at the office. If someone asks you for a piece of work which you know you cannot do within the timescale they give you, you will need to manage that and talk to them about it. You've learnt to manage people, situations and life at university and in your past life experience.

Develop your ability to handle people

1 Identify your boundaries in any relationship – the rules you feel comfortable with and stick to them.
2 Look at things from the other person's point of view. Put yourself in their shoes to get an idea for how they are feeling.
3 Remember that you cannot change other people – but you certainly *can* change the way you behave towards them.
4 Work on what you know you *can* influence, as opposed to the things you cannot.

Use your resources effectively

We have a tremendous amount of resources at our disposal, from mind-mapping to help creativity, speed reading to enable us to acquire knowledge more quickly, our memory to help retain it, meditation to help us focus and exercise to boost our energy. But the thing most people want more of today is time.

Is your time management letting you down?

'I haven't got time', is a common complaint. And yet how often do you reassess the way in which you spend your time (and money)?

- Track the ways in which you spend your time;
- Look back at your wheel of life and the activities you identified as important to you;
- How much of the 168 hours a week do you spend on them?
- Decide what to do about any imbalance;
- Track the way you spend your time for a week. In particular, track the time you're wasting on any of the activities in Table 10.4 below.

Table 10.4

Negative people/thoughts	Missing deadlines
Unanswered messages	Difficulty communicating
Outstanding letters and bills	Computer illiterate
Lacking confidence	Non-assertiveness
Unnecessary texting/emailing	Information overload
Losing things, e.g. keys	Smoking
Surfing the Internet	Drink and drugs
Broken items	Gambling
Too much TV	Fears
Poor sleep	Anxieties
Flitting from one thing to another	Doubts
without any real focus	Unnecessary meetings

Identify the three which waste most time for you and how much time they take up. What difference would it make if you didn't spend time on them? What are you going to do to get rid of them and what will you do with your time instead?

Undertake exercises like this while you're still at university, when you've graduated and later on when you have work, family and house maintenance responsibilities, when you are commuting and studying for professional qualifications, and have social and leisure activities to fit in. You can also apply it to your working day to find out how you can use your time more effectively at work.

Do the same exercise with money

- What financial base do you want to build up in the future?
- What do you need to do to make that happen?
- What is getting in the way?

Identify the financial resources you want and then you can start making them happen. Some items are essentials, such as a property to rent or buy, living costs and tax and state demands, e.g. national insurance. After that, saving is usually a wise move for that rainy day, and so is insurance. There are also a whole range of investments, savings accounts, stocks and shares which are best discussed with a financial adviser.

Ten ways to review your finances continually

1   Where is your money going?
2   Which items are essential, important, nice to have?

3 Where can you cut back?
4 What will you do to make that happen?
5 Which items do you no longer need and could sell?
6 How could you make more money? Examples include focusing on career development so that your salary increases.
7 Who can help you sort out your debts and finances?
8 What do banks and building societies offer graduates?
9 What realistically can you achieve in the next week, six months and three to five years? How can you capitalise on that? Put any unexpected windfalls such as a bonus or present into paying off your loan straight away.
10 How rigorously are you making your money work for you? How much attention are you paying to your current financial position?

Make your money work for you. Be proactive in looking for the best deal, the highest interest rates which suit your needs, the lowest loan rates, and keep looking. Do a three-monthly financial MOT and reward yourself for your financial acumen. The higher you climb the career ladder, the greater the perks and salary. Working for professional qualifications at night will not only boost your employability but also keep you away from expensive bars and nightclubs, keep your money in your pocket and enable you to pay off your loans and debts faster.

Most people continually believe they are short of time and money, but don't proactively do enough specifically about it. It takes discipline, effort and creative thinking to sort out your finances. Paying off a loan doesn't take forever, even though it may seem like it. Much depends on *how* focused you are in paying off your loans. And if you nurture your career, your financial status should get better as you're rewarded for your efforts. Careers take up around 48 weeks a year out of 52 and subsequently impact on your overall quality of life, so surely they are worth the effort and dedication?

Living at home with your parents after university?

Many young people are moving back home after university to save money, to pay off debts and for an assortment of other reasons. But what other options do you have apart from moving back in with your parent(s)? Could you get in touch with other graduates in the area or on the same graduate trainee scheme in your company who are in the same boat and flat-share, or live abroad in a country where graduates are welcomed and it is easier to get on the housing ladder? If you still decide to return home (perhaps you never left), work out a financial arrangement so that you pay your parent(s) rent (even if it is a very small amount) – you need to keep in the habit of budgeting for your housing. And arrange with them what your contribution will be towards the house-keeping, be it cleaning, washing, helping in the garden, cooking a meal a couple of times a week. Don't fall back into the ways of a teenager having everything done for you. You've moved on from that and so have your parents, so don't use your parents' home: sit up, take some responsibility and *contribute* to it. Sit down and agree a few house rules (just as you would have had at university with your flat mates) to keep everyone happy and remember to practice the art of negotiation and compromise. Finally, consider these questions:

- How long do you intend to stay with your parents? Give yourself a deadline to leave and stick to it. Do you want to be living with them when you're 40?
- How much of your student debt will you have paid off by that time? How will you do it?
- What will you have achieved in your career by then and how will that have boosted your income to help you start building a financial base?

Finally, when the time does come to move out, why not get your parents a small gift as a token of appreciation for their help over the years? Parents are usually very happy to help out their offspring – but it is always nice to be appreciated and thanked.

Don't forget the wild and wacky

What would your life be like if you drew up a list of all the things you wanted to do and achieved before your eightieth birthday? What a glorious blaze of memories you could have to look back on as your older years set in!

List the things you want to do and the reasons *not* to do them will fade into the background. You'll be filled with a tremendous energy and enthusiasm, passion and excitement as you start identifying how and when you're going to do it all. Writing your list down enhances your determination to make your items happen. Keep your list where you can easily see it *frequently*. Show your list to those who are important to you in your life. Suggest they draw up a list of their own, and compare notes. Are there things you can do together? Can you give each other the time and space required to them happen? You need to make sure that those you love don't constrain you in a plant pot, so that your roots can't spread out and grow. If they do limit you, it may be time to say farewell to the relationship. A rich relationship should enable you to take some journeys as a couple and others alone.

Don't become a robot

It's easy to fall into a continuous cycle of work, supper, TV, bed. The more you do, the more you'll want to do and the dream list above can help you do just that! And as you push back your boundaries outside work, it will also become much easier to do just that in your working life. At the start of this book, you identified what success and happiness meant to you. Perhaps you listed things like a large bank account, exotic holidays, happy, healthy kids who stay off drugs and alcohol; giving something back to the community which really makes a difference, a particular status in the community or organisation.

You need to decide how important success is to you and in what capacity. Occasionally, you may tweak or transform your ideas of success and happiness or completely change them. But in the hustle, bustle and noise of life, take time out to dream and look into the present and future to ensure you're spending your life on activities which, and with people who, are important to you. Get focused and create the life and success you want.

Looking forward

The goal posts of life are for your own positioning. Be clear about the things you want to change in your life and what you want out of it, and then take personal responsibility to make it happen. You may need to work around barriers and obstacles, and take regulations and rules into account along the way, but the journey makes the end achievement all the more rewarding.

Your degree over, you have a chance to look back, contemplate, reflect and congratulate yourself, and to look forward, to plan and build your future. Pause to do this at regular intervals in your life and it will feature the activities and achievements which are important to you.

Finally, consider what really is important in life. Do any of these elements feature for you?

1   Love and be loved;
2   Be passionate about a cause;
3   Wonder at the beauty of the earth and nature's sheer power;
4   Feel at peace;
5   Laugh and see the funny side;
6   Care for those you know and those you don't;
7   Be curious: don't lose the habit of asking what, why, when, where, who, how;
8   Learn from those who've gone before you and who'll come after you;
9   Use your creativity and imagination to the full;
10   Create you own luck, success and happiness.

Summary action points

Your life
Your future
Your choice
Good luck!

Further reading

Careers related

Alexander, L. (2003) *Turn Redundancy to Opportunity*, Oxford: How To Books Ltd.

Barrett, J. and Williams, G. (2003) *Test Your Own Aptitude*, London: Kogan Page Ltd.

Fishman, T.C. (2005) *China Inc*, London: Simon & Schuster UK Ltd.

Davis, J. and Lambert, R. (2002): *Engineering in Emergencies – A Practical Guide for Relief Workers*, London: ITDG Publishing.

GTI Target: published by GTI Specialist Publishers (www.groupgti.com) including:
* Civil and Structural Engineering
* Construction and Building Services
* Engineering.

Get Engineering, published by Hobsons.

Lees, J. (2005) *How to Get a Job You'll Love*, London: McGraw-Hill.

Williams, N. (2004), *The Work We Were Born to Do*, London: Element Books Ltd.

Further study

Marshall, S. and Green, N. (2004) *Your PhD Companion*, Oxford: How To Books Ltd. Contains a great selection of tips and advice to help you through your PhD.

Recruitment

See the website www.alec.co.uk for lots of formats and examples of CVs.

Bishop-Firth, R. (2004) *CVs for High Flyers*, Oxford: How To Books Ltd.

Bryon, M. (2005) *Graduate Psychometric Test Workbook*, London: Kogan Page Ltd.

Johnstone, J. (2005) *Pass that Interview: Your Systematic Guide to Coming Out On Top*, Oxford: How To Books Ltd.

Yate, M.J. (2002) *The Ultimate CV Book*, London: Kogan Page Ltd.

Yate, M.J. (2003) *The Ultimate Job Search Letters Page*, London: Kogan Page Ltd.

Yate, M.J. (2005) *Great Answers to Tough Interview Questions*, London: Kogan Page Ltd.

Moving up the career ladder

Bishop-Firth, R. (2004) *The Ultimate CV for Managers and Professionals*, Oxford: How To Books Ltd.

Hughes, V. (2004) *Becoming a Director*, Oxford: How To Books Ltd.

Purkiss, J. and Edlmair, B (2005) *How To Be Headhunted*, Oxford: How To Books Ltd.

Shavick, A. (2005) *Management Level Psychometric and Assessment Tests*, Oxford: How To Books Ltd.

Working abroad

Carte, P. and Fox, C. (2004) *Bridging the Culture Gap: A Practical Guide to International Business Communication*, London: Kogan Page Ltd.

Doing Business With, an excellent series published by Kogan Page Ltd covering these countries: Bahrain, Croatia, Saudi Arabia, UAE, China, Jordon, Kazakhstan, Kuwait, Lybia, Serbia and Montenegro and the EU Accession States.

Going to Live in ...and *Living and Working in* ...two highly informative and practical series published by How To Books Ltd (Oxford), covering countries such as Spain, Australia, New Zealand, France, Italy and Greece.

Khan-Panni, P. and Swallow, D. (2003) *Communicating Across Cultures*, Oxford: How To Books Ltd.

Reuvid, J. (2006) *Working Abroad: The Complete Guide to Overseas Employment*, London: Kogan Page Ltd.

Vacation Work have a plethora of publications which give you ideas on how you can go and work your way around the world. Visit www.vacationwork.co.uk.

Self-employment

Blackwell, E. (2004) *How to Prepare a Business Plan*, London: Kogan Page Ltd.

Bridge, R. (2004) *How I Made It: 40 Entrepreneurs Reveal All*, London: Kogan Page Ltd.

Gray, D. (2004) *Start and Run a Profitable Consultancy Business*, London: Kogan Page Ltd.

Isaacs, B. (2004) *Work For Yourself and Reap the Rewards*, Oxford: How To Books Ltd.

Jolly, A. (2005) *From Idea to Profit*, London: Kogan Page Ltd.

Power, P. (2005) *The Kitchen Table Entrepreneur*, Oxford: How To Books Ltd. Turn that hobby into a profitable business!

Reuvid, J. (2006) *Start Up and Run Your Own Business*, London: Kogan Page Ltd.

Whiteley, J. (2003) *Going for Self-Employment*, Oxford: How To Books Ltd.

Gap year/time out

Potter, R. (2004) *Worldwide Volunteering*, Oxford: How To Books Ltd.

Vandome, N. (2005) *Planning Your Gap Year*, Oxford: How To Books Ltd.

Career and life success

Drummond, N. (2005) *The Spirit of Success*, London: Hodder and Stoughton.

Ebury, S. (2003) *Moving On Up*, London: Ebury Press.

Hill, N. (1996) *Think and Grow Rich*, New York: Ballantine Books.

Robbins, A. (1991) *Awaken the Giant Within*, New York: Simon and Schuster.

Tracy, B. (2003) *Goals! How to Get Everything You Want – Faster Than You Ever Thought Possible*, San Francisco: Berrett-Koehler Publishers Inc.

Learning skills

Bradbury, A. (2006) *Successful Presentation Skills*, London: Kogan Page Ltd.

Claston, G. and Lucas, B. (2004) *Be Creative*, London: BBC Books Ltd.

Covey, S. (2005) *The 7 Habits of Highly Effective People: Powerful Lessons in Personal Change*, London: Simon & Schuster UK Ltd.

Lilley, R. (2006) *Dealing with Difficult People*, London, Kogan Page Ltd.

Parsloe, E. (1999) *The Manager as Coach and Mentor*, London, CIPD.

Quillam, S. (2003) *What Makes People Tick?* London: Element.

Wiseman, Dr R. (2004) *The Luck Factor: Change Your Luck – and Change Your Life*, Sydney: Random House Australia (Pty) Ltd.

Managing others

Charney, C. (2001) *Your Instant Adviser: The A–Z of Getting Ahead in the Workplace*, London: Kogan Page Ltd.

Morris, M.J. (2005) *The First-Time Manager*, London: Kogan Page Ltd.

Taylor, D. (2005) *The Naked Leader*, London: Bantam Books.

Whitmore, J. (2002) *Coaching for Performance*, London: Nicholas Brealey Publishing.

Building financial bases

Ahuja, A. (2004) *The First-time Buyer's Guide*, Oxford: How To Books Ltd.

Bowley, G. (2005) *Making Your Own Will*, Oxford: How To Books Ltd.

Chesworth, N. (2004) *The Complete Guide to Buying and Renting Your First Home*, London: Kogan Page Ltd.

Palmer, T. (2005) *Getting Out of Debt and Staying Out*, Oxford: How To Books Ltd.

Life related

Fortgang, L.B. (2002) *Take Yourself to the Top*, London: Thorsons.

Gaskell, C. (2000) *Transform Your Life – 10 Steps to Real Results*, London: Thorsons.

Useful addresses and further information

UK general

Association of Graduate Careers Advisory Services
Administration Office
Millennium House
30 Junction Road
Sheffield S11 8XB
Tel: 0114 251 5750
www.agcas.org.uk

Hobsons
www.hobsons.com
A website with lots of features to help you get that right job wherever you are

Prospects
www.prospects.ac.uk
A huge source of information and useful links for graduates of every discipline

UK regional graduate websites

Many of the sites below are designed to help graduates returning to the region or wishing to move to the area:
Yorkshire and Humber Region: www.graduatelink.com
Graduates Yorkshire: www.graduatesyorkshire.info
Graduates North East: www.graduates.northeast.ac.uk
Merseyside-Business Bridge www.business-bridge.org.uk
Merseyside: www.gieu.co.uk
Merseyside Workplace: www.merseyworkplace.com/
North West Student and Graduate On-Line: www.nwsago.co.uk

North Midlands and Cheshire Employers Directory: www.soc.
staffs.ac.uk/eh1/emp2003.html
Staffordshire Graduate Link: www.staffsgradlink.co.uk
Graduate Advantage – West Midlands: www.graduateadvantage.
co.uk
Gradsouthwest.com: www.gradsouthwest.com
GradsEast: www.gradseast.org.uk
The Careers Group, University of London: www.careers.lon.ac.uk
Graduate Ireland: www.gradireland.com
Scotland Graduate Careers, managed by Services to Graduates
Group: www.graduatecareers-scotland.org
Scotland – Graduates for Growth: www.graduatesforgrowth.co.uk
GO Wales: www.gowales.co.uk

Work experience, internships and voluntary work

Do It!
www.do-it.org
Find out what opportunities there are to volunteer in the region
you live in

Everything you wanted to Know
www.everythingyouwantedtoknow.com
Undergraduate work placement and sponsorship

GO Wales
www.gowales.co.uk

Graduate Business Partnership
run by the University of Exeter
www.ex.ac.uk/businessprojects

Knowledge Transfer Partnership
www.ktponline.org.uk/graduates

Merseyside-Business Bridge
www.business-bridge.org.uk

www.gieu.co.uk
Merseyside-related programme of events to enhance your employability and prepare you for a competitive job market with repre-
sentatives from various sectors

National Council for Work Experience
Tel: 0845 601 5510
www.work-experience.org
enquiries@work-experience.org

Shell Technology Enterprise Programme (STEP)
www.step.org.uk
For students in their second or penultimate year at university, the chance to take part in placements with small and medium-sized businesses

West Midlands Graduate Advantage
www.graduateadvantage.co.uk

Year in Industry
www.yini.org.uk

Further study

Association of MBAs
25 Hosier Lane
London EC1A 9LQ
Tel: 0207 246 2686
www.mbaworld.com
Has a full list of accredited MBA courses, plus links to institutions, and details of the MBA fair, scholarships, awards loans. The Official MBA Handbook can be acquired over their site and gives you all the information you need to get started. There's also information about rankings

British Council
10 Spring Gardens
London SW1A 2BN
Tel: 0161 857 7755 (Information centre)
www.britcoun.org
The British Council has a network of offices throughout the UK and in 110 countries worldwide. Visit its website or one of its offices for more information on funding, scholarships and studying in the UK. You will also find a lot of information about Arts, Science and Society in the UK

National Union of Students
www.nusonline.co.uk

Ploteus
www.europa.eu.int/ploteus
The European course search portal

National Post-Graduate Committee
www.npc.org.uk
The NCP represents the interests of post-graduate students in the UK. Information on funding, discussion boards, post-graduate facts and issues, and post-graduate careers. Also an academic job search with international links to jobs in the USA, Canada and Australia among others

Prospects
www.prospects.ac.uk
Everything you want to know about post-graduate study!

UKNARIC
Oriel House
Oriel Road
Cheltenham
Gloucestershire GL50 1XP
Tel: 0870 990 4088
www.naric.org.uk
The National Recognition Centre for the UK and National Agency for the Department for Education and Skills. The only official information provider on the comparability of international qualifications from over 180 countries

www.postgrad.hobsons.com
A programme search, study and life

www.studyuk.hobsons.com
For the student who wants to study in the UK

www.mba.hobsons.com
The complete guide to MBAs

UKCOSA
www.ukcosa.org.uk
Lots of information for students wishing to come to the UK to study

Research

British Academy
www.britac.ac.uk
Directory of post-graduate studentships in scientific research
www.newscientistjobs.com

Engineering Professors' Council
www.engprofc.ac.uk/

European Science Foundation
www.esf.org

European Society for Engineering Education
www.ntb.ch/sefi/

Engineering and Physical Sciences Research Council
www.epsrc.ac.uk

European Council of Applied Sciences, Technologies and Engineering
Euro-CASE
28 Rue Saint Dominique
F-75007 Paris
Tel: +33 1 53 59 53 40
www.euro-case.org
Provides independent advice on engineering research, development and the resultant technology

Find a PhD
www.FindAPhD.com
This website is the largest directory of PhD opportunities in the UK

Higher Education and Research Opportunities in the United Kingdom
www.hero.ac.uk
An excellent section on research with links to the main research councils, universities and others. Plus information on how to disclose your findings as a new researcher

National Academy of Engineering
www.nae.edu

National Endowment for Science, Technology and the Arts
www.nesta.org.uk

Office of Science and Technology
www.dti.gov.uk/ost

Research Councils
www.research-councils.ac.uk
A partnership set up to promote science, engineering and technology supported by the eight UK Research Councils. Grants are allocated to individual researchers, networks of people working on projects, programmes, designated research centres, fellowships and post-graduate students

The Royal Academy of Engineering
29 Great Peter Street
London SW1P 3LW
Tel: 0207 227 0500
www.raeng.org.uk/research/researcher/default.htm
Find out more about the Best Programme which provides education and training opportunities that can be accessed throughout your career

The Royal Society
www.royalsoc.ac.uk

The United Kingdom Research Office (UKRO)
www.ukro.ac.uk
The leading information and advice service on EU funding for research and higher education

Universities UK
www.universitiesuk.ac.uk

Self-employment

British Franchise Association
Thames View
Newton Road
Henley-on-Thames
Oxon RH9 1HG
Tel: 01491 578 050
www.thebfa.org

For information on franchises, both in and outside the UK, finding a franchise, successful case studies and events, a list of members. Ask for a copy of the British Franchise Association Franchisee Information Pack and check when the next Franchise Exhibition is near you on its website

BusinessLink
www.businesslink.gov.uk
A network of business advice centres in England with allied bodies in Scotland, Wales and Northern Ireland, all accessible through this site

Prime Initiative
Astral House
1268 London Road
London SW16 4ER
Tel: 0208 765 7833
www.primeinitiative.org.uk/
Dedicated to helping those over 50 to set up their own business

Prince's Trust
Tel: 0800 842 842
www.princes-trust.org.uk
Help for the 14–30 year old who wants to set up his or her own business or tackle barriers to employment

Shell LiveWIRE
www.shell-livewire.org/
Unlock your potential with this excellent site. Plus financial action planning and a fabulous business encyclopaedia. For 16–30 year olds who want to start and develop their own business

Start-ups
www.startups.co.uk

Patents

Chartered Institute of Patent Agents
95 Chancery Lane
London WC2A 1DT
Tel: 0207 405 9450
www.cipa.org.uk

Patent Office
Concept House
Cardiff Road
Newport NP10 8QQ
Tel: 0845 9500 505
www.patent.gov.uk

Job sites

These sector specific sites may also be useful:

Animated People
www.animatedpeople.com

Careers in Construction
www.careersinconstruction.com

Chemical Engineer
www.chemicalengineer.com

Civil Engineering Jobs
www.civilengineeringjobs.com

Just Engineers
www.justengineers.net

Mechanical Engineer
www.mechanicalengineer.com/

Oil Career
www.oilcareers.com

Primavera
www.primavera.org

Project Management
www.project-management-jobs.com

Telecommunication Engineer
www.telecommunication.engineer.jobs.com

UK Civil Engineering
www.ukcivilengineering.com

Technology horizons
www.technologyhorizons.com

Thomas Telford
www.t-telford.co.uk/recruitment

The Engineer Online
www.theengineer.co.uk

Universities, colleges and schools

www.jobs.ac.uk
The official recruitment website for staffing in higher education

www.jobs.tes.co.uk
The *Times Educational Supplement* with lots of vacancies in education

Working abroad

Dangerzone Jobs
www.dangerzonejobs.com
Jobs in dangerous areas

Engineering without Borders
www.ewb-usa.com/index.php
USA-based organisation which works with developing communities to improve the quality of life through engineering projects with students and professional engineers.

Out of the ordinary
www.dfes.gov.uk/europeopen
For those people living in the EU who want to work in other countries there

Professional bodies

Construction Industry Council
26 Store Street
London WC1E 7BT
Tel: 0207 399 7400
www.cic.org.uk
This site has a huge range of links, both national and international

Cogent
www.cogent-ssc.com
Sector Skills Council for the oil and gas, chemicals manufacturing
and petroleum industries

Construction Skills
www.constructionskills.net
Construction Skills is the Sector Skills Council for construction in
the UK and it consists of a partnership between the CITB, Construction Skills, the Construction Industry Council and the CITB
Northern Ireland

European Construction Institute
Sir Frank Gibb Annexe
West Park
Loughborough University
Loughborough LE11 3TU
Tel: 01509 223 526
www.eci-online.org

Engineering Construction Industry Association
Broadway House
Tothill Street
London SW1H 9NS
Tel: 0207 799 2000
www.ecia.co.uk
Supports and promotes the UK engineering construction industry

Engineering Employers Federation
Broadway House
Tothill Street
London SW1H 9NQ
Tel: 0207 222 7777
www.eef.co.uk
Provides advice and services to businesses, e.g. environment, health
and safety, HR and legal, training, information and research,
manufacturing matters

Engineering and Technology Board
10 Maltravers Street
London WC2R 3ER
Tel: 0207 240 7333
www.etechb.co.uk

Engineering Construction Industry Training Board
Blue Court
Church Lane
Kings Langley
Herts WDE4 8JP
Tel: 01923 260 000
www.ecitb.org.uk

Engineering Council
10 Maltravers Street
London WC2R 3ER
Tel: 0207 240 7891
www.engc.org.uk

Standards and Routes to Registration
www.engc.org.uk/Registration/Registration_Process.aspx

International Register of Professional Engineers
www.iee.org/professionalregistration/IRoPE.cfm

International Engineering Agreements
www.ieagreements.com/
Six agreements govern the mutual recognition of professional
qualifications and competence. Find out more here about the
Washington Accord, the Dublin Accord, The Sydney Accord, the
Engineers' Mobility Forum, the APEC Engineer Agreement and the
Engineering Technologist Mobility Forum. There are also exam-
ples of graduate and professional competence profiles

Engineering Careers Information Service
SEMTA
14 Upton Road
Watford
Hertfordshire WD1 7EP
www.semta.org.uk

Scottish Engineering
105 West George Street
Glasgow G2 1QL
Tel: 0141 221 3181
www.scottishengineering.org.uk

Sector Skills Council for Science, Engineering and Manufacturing Technologies
14 Upton Road
Watford WD18 0JT
www.semta.org.uk
www.elip.info is the Engineering Learning Information Portal for details on learning opportunities in the UK.

Skillset
Prospect House
80–110 New Oxford Street
London WC1A 1MB
Tel: 0207 520 5757
www.skillset.org
The sector skills council for the audio-visual industries

SummitSkills Ltd
Vega House
Opal Drive
Fox Milne
Milton Keynes MK15 0DF
Tel: 01908 303960
www.summitskills.org.uk
enquiries@summitskills.org.uk
The sector skills council for the building services engineering sector.

Professional organisations and trade associations

The following are examples of professional and trade associations which relate to business and finance. Many have international links with their peers abroad, so research their websites thoroughly.

International organisations

Asian Federation of Engineering Organisations
www.aseanengineers.com/index.html

Commonwealth Engineers' Council
www.ice.org.uk/cec
Links to the various Institutions of Engineers

Engineers Australia
www.ieaust.org.au

European Federation of National Engineering Associations
www.feani.org

Institute of Electrical and Electronics Engineers
www.ieee.org/portal
365,000 members in over 150 countries with over 1,300 student branches at universities in 80 countries

National Society for Professional Engineers
www.nspe.org

World Federation of Engineering Organisations
www.unesco.org/wfeo
Brings together national engineering organisations from over 90 countries and represents some eight million engineers around the world.

Professional bodies (many with international links)

These are by no means inclusive and you should make liberal use of the links pages on sites to really ensure you find the most appropriate body for you and your career plans

Acoustics

Institute of Acoustics
77A St Peter's Street
St Albans
Hertfordshire AL1 3BN
Tel: 01727 848 195
www.ioa.org.uk

Aerospace

Civil Aviation Authority
45–59 Kingsway
London WC2B 6TE
Tel: 0207 379 7311
www.caa.co.uk

National Air Traffic Services
4000 Parkway
Whiteley
Fareham
Hants PO15 7FL
Tel: 01489 616001
Freephone: 0800 068 8299
www.nats.co.uk

Royal Aeronautical Society
4 Hamilton Place
London W1J 7BQ
Tel: 0207 670 4326
www.aerosociety.com

British Women Pilots Association
Brooklands Museum
Brooklands Road
Weybridge
Surrey KT13 0QN
www.bwpa.co.uk

Agricultural

Institution of Agricultural Engineers
West End Road
Silsoe
Bedford MK45 4DU
Tel: 01525 861 096
www.iagre.org
secretary@iagre.org

Architecture

American Institute of Architects
www.aia.org

Australian Institute of Landscape Architects
www.aila.org.au

Architects' Registration Board (ARB)
8 Weymouth Street
London W1N 3FB
Tel: 0207 580 5861
www.arb.org.uk
info@arb.org.uk

Royal Incorporation of Architects in Scotland (RIAS)
15 Rutland Square
Edinburgh EH1 2BE
Tel: 0131 229 7545
www.rias.org.uk
info@rias.org.uk

British Institute of Architectural Technologists (BIAT)
397 City Road
London EC1V 1NH
Tel: 0207 278 2206
www.biat.org.uk
careers@biat.org.uk

Landscape Institute
33 Great Portland Street
London W1W 8QG
Tel: 0207 299 4500
www.landscapeinstitute.org
Produce a careers pack.
mail@landscapeinstitute.org

Royal Institute of British Architects (RIBA)
Public Information Line
66 Portland Place
London W1B 1AD
Tel: 0207 580 5533
www.architecture.com
info@inst.riba.org
Visit www.riba-jobs.com for more information about vacancies

Royal Institution of Naval Architects
10 Upper Belgrave Street
London SW1X 8BQ
Tel: 0207 235 8622
ww.rina.org.uk
hq@rina.org.uk

Armed forces

Army Recruiting Group
Tel: 08457 300 111
www.army.mod.uk

Royal Air Force
www.raf.mod.uk/careers.html

Royal Navy
www.royal-navy.mod.uk

Built environment

Association of Building Engineers (ABE)
Lutyens House
Billing Brook Road
Weston Favell
Northampton NN3 8NW
Tel: 0845 126 1058
www.abe.org.uk
building.engineers@abe.org.uk

Building Conservation
Cathedral Communications Ltd
High Street
Tisbury
Wiltshire SP3 6HA
Tel: 01747 871717
www.buildingconservation.com
Internet sister to the Building Conservation Directory, with information on events and exhibitions worldwide plus recruitment and articles plus list of undergraduate and post-graduate courses

Building and Estates Forum – Constructing Excellence in the Built Environment
PO Box 2874
London Road
Reading RG1 5UQ
Tel: 0870 922 0034
www.constructingexcellence.org.uk

Chartered Institute of Building
Englemere
King's Ride
Ascot
Berkshire SL5 7TB
Tel: 01344 630 700
www.ciob.org.uk

Chartered Institution of Building Services Engineers
222 Balham High Road
London SW12 9BS
Tel: 0208 675 5211
www.cibse.org
info@cibse.org

Commission for Architecture and the Built Environment (CABE)
1 Kemble Street
London WC2B 4AN
Tel: 0207 070 6700
www.cabe.org.uk

Institute of Historic Building Conservation
www.ihbc.org.uk
The professional body for building conservation in the UK with lots of invaluable links

Institute of Building Control
92–104 East Street
Epsom
Surrey KT17 1EB
Tel: 0207 222 7000
www.building-control.org

International Society of the Built Environment
Postfach 9
CH-4466
Ormalingen
Switzerland
www.isbe.demon.co.uk/index.html

Resource for Urban Design Information (RUDI)
Oxford Brookes University
Gipsy Lane
Headington
Oxford OX3 OPB
Tel: 01865 483 602
www.rudi.net

The Society of Environmental Engineers
The Manor House
High Street
Buntingford
Herts SG9 9AB
Tel: 01763 271209
www.environmental.org.uk

Chemical engineering

American Institute of Chemical Engineers
3 Park Avenue
New York 10016-5991
USA
Tel: +1 800 242 4363
www.aiche.org

Biomedical Engineering
www.bmes.org

The Biomedical Engineering Network
www.bmenet.org/BMEnet

Biomedical and Clinical Engineering portal
www.ebme.co.uk

Chemical Engineering (magazine)
www.che.com

International Federation for Medical and Biological Engineering
www.ifmbe.org

Institution of Chemical Engineers
Davis Building
165–189 Railway Terrace
Rugby CV21 3HQ
Tel: 01788 578214
www.icheme.org

www.ciw.uni-karlsruhe.de/chem-eng.html
An international directory of chemical engineering sites all over
the world, including newsgroups, research, laboratories, chemical
companies and commercial organisations

The Chemical Institute of Canada
130 Rue Slater Street
Ottawa, Ontario K1P 6E2
Tel: +1 613 232 6252
www.chemeng.ca

World Chemical Engineering Council
www.chemengcouncil.org

Civil and structural engineering

Chartered Institution of Water and Environmental Management
15 John Street
London WC1N 2EB
Tel: 0207 831 3110
www.ciwem.org.uk

Chinese Hydraulic Engineering Society
www.ches.org.cn

The Internet for the Civil Engineer
www.icivilengineer.com
News, careers, project watch, recruitment plus free magazines and
careers fairs

Institution of Civil Engineers
1 Great George Street
Westminster
London SW1P 3AA
Tel: 0207 222 7722
www.ice.org.uk

Institution of Civil Engineering Surveyors
Dominion House
Sibson Road
Sale
Cheshire M33 7PP
www.ices.org.uk

Institution of Fire Engineers
London Road
Moreton-in-Marsh
Gloucestershire GL56 0RH
Tel: 01608 812580
www.ife.org.uk
info@ife.org.uk

Institution of Highway Incorporated Engineers
De Morgan House
58 Russell Square
London WC1B 4HS
Tel: 0207 436 7487
www.ihie.org.uk

Institution of Structural Engineers
11 Upper Belgrave Street
London SW1X 8BH
Tel: 0207 235 4535
www.istructe.org.uk

The Water Page
www.thewaterpage.com
Dedicated to the promotion of sustainable water management with lots of useful international links to agencies, bodies and companies working with water

Computing

British Computer Society
1st Floor, Block D
North Star House
North Star Avenue
Swindon SN2 1FA
Tel: 01793 417 417
www.bsc.org.uk

Entertainment Leisure Software Publishers Association
www.elspa.com

UK Web Design Association
Fareham Enterprise Centre
Hackett Way
Fareham
Hampshire PO14 1TH
www.ukwda.org

Design

Design Council
34 Bow Street
London WC2E 7DL
Tel: 0207 420 5200
www.design-council.org.uk
www.yourcreativefuture.org

Institution of Engineering Designers
Courtleigh
Westbury Leigh
Westbury
Wiltshire BA13 3TA
Tel: 01373 822801
www.ied.org.uk

The following sites may also be useful:
www.britishdesign.co.uk: British Design Innovation
www.bedg.org: British European Design Group
www.cfsd.org.uk: Centre for Sustainable Design
www.dba.org.uk: Design Business Association
www.designinbusiness.org.uk: Design in Business
wwwdesignmuseum.org: Design Museum
www.designresearchsociety.org: Design Research Society
www.dffn.org: Design for Future Needs
www.hhrc.rca.ac.uk: Helen Hamlyn Research Centre
www.interiordesignhandbook.com: Interior Design Handbook

Estate agents

National Association of Estate Agents
Arbon House
21 Jury Street
Warwick CV34 4EH
Tel: 01926 496 800
www.naea.co.uk
info@naea.co.uk

Engineering

Association of Consulting Engineers
Alliance House
12 Caxton Street
London SW1H 0QL
Tel: 0207 222 6557
www.acenet.co.uk

Association of Consulting Engineers, Australia
www.acea.com.au

Energy

Council for Registered Gas Installers (CORGI)
1 Elmwood
Chineham Park
Crockford Lane
Basingstoke
Hants RH24 8WG
www.corgi-gas.com
enquiries@corgi-gas.com

British Nuclear Energy Society
At the ICE
1–7 Great George Street
London SW1P 3AA
Tel: 0207 222 7722
www.bnes.com

Energy and Utility Skills
Friars Gate Two
1011 Stratford Road
Shirley
Solihull B90 4BN
Tel: 0845 077 9922
www.euskills.co.uk

Energy Institute
61 New Cavendish Street
London W1G 7AR
Tel: 0207 467 7100
www.energyinst.org.uk
info@energyinst.org.uk

Institution of Chemical Engineers
Davis Building
165–189 Railway Terrace
Rugby CV21 3HQ
Tel: 01788 578 214
www.icheme.org.uk

Institution of Gas Engineers and Managers
Charnwood Wing
Ashby Road
Loughborough
Leicestershire LE11 3GR
Tel: 01509 282728
www.igem.org.uk

Institution of Nuclear Engineers
Allan House
1 Penerley Road
London SW6 2LQ
Tel: 0208 698 1500
www.inuce.org.uk
inucewh@aol.com

Electrical engineers

Institution of Engineering and Technology
Savoy Place
London WC2R 0BL
Tel: 0207 240 1871
www.theiet.org

Health and safety

Royal Society for the Prevention of Accidents
RoSPA House
Edgbaston Park
353 Bristol Road
Birmingham B5 7ST
Tel: 0121 248 2000
www.rospa.com

British Safety Council
70 Chancellor's Road
London W6 9RS
Tel: 0208 741 1231
www.britishsafetycouncil.co.uk

Health and Safety Executive
Redgrave Court
Bootle
Merseyside L20 3QZ
Tel: 0845 345 0055
www.hse.gov.uk

Marine

Careers in Shipping
Carthusian Court
12 Carthusian Street
London EC1M 6EZ
Tel: 0800 085 0973
www.gotosea.org.uk

International Marine Contractors Association
5 Lower Belgrave Street
London SW1W 0NR
Tel: 0207 824 5520
www.imca-int.com
imca@imca-int.com

Institute of Marine Engineering, Science and Technology
(IMarEST)
80 Coleman Street
London EC2R 5BJ
Tel: 0207 382 2600
www.imarest.org
info@imarest.org

Merchant Navy Training Board
Carthusian Court
12 Carthusian Street
London EC1M 6EZ
Tel: 0207 417 2800
www.mntb.org
enquiry@mntb.org

Materials, minerals and mining

Institute of Cast Metal Engineers
National Metalforming Centre
47 Birmingham Road
West Bromwich
West Midlands B70 6PY
Tel: 0121 601 6979
www.icme.org.uk
info@icme.org.uk

Institute of Materials, Minerals and Mining (IOM)
1 Carlton House Terrace
London SW1Y 5DB
Tel: 0207 451 7300
www.iom3.org

Mechanical engineering

American Society of Mechanical Engineers
www.asme.org

Institution of Mechanical Engineers
1 Birdcage Walk
London SW1H 9JJ
Tel: 0207 222 7899
www.imeche.org.uk

Measurement and control

Institute of Measurement and Control
87 Gower Street
London WC1E 6AF
Tel: 0207 398 4949
www.instmc.org.uk

Multimedia

British Interactive Multimedia Association
Briarlea house
Southend Road
Billericay CM11 2PR
www.bima.co.uk
info@bima.co.uk

BBC Recruitment Services
PO Box 48305
London W12 6YE
www.bbc.co.uk/jobs

British Kinematograph Sound and Television Society
The Moving Image Society
Pinewood Studios
Iver Heath
Bucks SL0 0NH
Tel: 01753 656 656

www.bksts.com
info@bksts.com

CFP Europe
Bernhard Bangs Allé 25
2000 Frederiksberg
Denmark
Tel: +45 33 86 28 91
www.cfp-e.com
cfp-e@cfp-e.com

Channel 4 Television
124 Horseferry Road
London SW1P 2TX
www.channel4.com
careers@channel4.co.uk

five tv
www.five.tv

British Film Institute
www.bfi.org.uk

ITV
ITV Network Centre
200 Gray's Inn Road
London EC1X 8HF
www.itv.com/jobs

Operations management

Society of Operations Engineering
22 Greencoat Place
London SW1P 1PR
Tel: 0207 630 1111
www.soe.org.uk
soe@soe.org.uk

Physics

Institute of Physics
76 Portland Place
London W1B 1NT
Tel: 0207 470 4800
www.iop.org
physics@iop.org

Project management

Association for Project Management
150 West Wycombe Road
High Wycombe
Buckinghamshire HP12 3AE
Tel: 0845 458 1944
www.apm.org.uk

Project Manager Today
www.pmtoday.co.uk/
Has an excellent page linking to international organisations

International Project Management Association
PO Box 1167
3860 BD Nijkerk
The Netherlands
Tel: +31 33 247 34 30
www.ipma.ch

International Cost Engineering Council
1168 Hidden Lake Drive
NC 28630
USA
Tel: +1 828 728 5287
www.icoste.org

Quarrying

Institute of Quarrying
7 Regent Street
Nottingham NG1 5BS
Tel: 0115 945 3880
www.quarrying.org
mail@quarrying.org

Surveying

Australian Institute of Quantity Surveyors
www.aiqs.com.au

Royal Institution of Chartered Surveyors
Surveyor Court
Westwood Way
Coventry CV4 8JE
Tel: 0870 333 1600
www.rics.org.uk

Recruitment

Recruitment and Employment Confederation
36–38 Mortimer Street
London W1N 7RB
Tel: 0207 462 3260
www.rec.uk.com

Space

Space Careers
www.space-careers.com
Excellent links to related associations and resources plus a space
industry directory and news. Space Careers is a free service offered
to job hunters by the consultancy company Spacelinks

Telecommunications

National Association of Radio and Telecommunications Engineers
www.narte.org/
A worldwide non-profit professional association

Transport

Go Skills
Concorde house
Trinity Park
Solihull
West Midlands B37 7UQ
Tel: 0121 635 5520
www.goskills.org
The sector skills council for passenger transport

ReMIT (Retail Motor Industry Training)
www.remit.co.uk

Women related sites

Women into Science, Engineering and Construction
22 Old Queen Street
London SW1H 9HP
Tel: 0207 227 8421
www.wisecampaign.org.uk

The Women's Engineering Society
Michael Faraday house
Six Hills Way
Stevenage
Herts SG1 2AY
Tel: 01438 765506
www.wes.org.uk

Printed in the United States
by Baker & Taylor Publisher Services